FROM
ENTREPRENEUR
TO EMPLOYER

Human Resources for Small Business in Ontario

Pamela Urie

For information contact:
http://www.urhr.ca

Front cover image: PeopleImages/E+/gettyimages

Printed in Canada
ISBN: 978-1-9992364-0-3

First Edition: November 2020

FIN 02 02 2021

DISCLAIMER

The author and all persons involved in the preparation and sale of this publication disclaim any warranty as to accuracy or currency of the publication. This publication is provided on the understanding and basis that none of the publisher, author, editor, or other persons involved in the creation of this publication shall be responsible for the accuracy or currency of the contents, or for the results of any action taken on the basis of the information contained in this publication, or for any errors or omissions contained herein.

No one involved in this publication is attempting herein to render legal, accounting, or other professional advice. If legal advice or other expert assistance is required, the services of a competent professional should be sought. The information contained herein should in no way be construed as being either official or unofficial policy of any governmental body.

This book is dedicated to my mother,
Sarah Dunn (Buchanan) Upfield
and to the memory of my father,
George Frederick James Upfield,
my earliest mentors and role models.

Acknowledgment

Many thanks to my husband, Gordon Urie, for his unfailing support and encouragement, and for his willingness to spend hours painstakingly critiquing my work.

Contents

Contents

Introduction

As a sole entrepreneur ready to expand your business, you are taking on a new challenge – that of hiring staff. You may be tempted to hurry the process, but before you begin, it is important to learn about effective employment practices.

You might have a small business that already has a workforce. Perhaps expansion and hiring have been haphazard. Job descriptions and reporting relationships may be informal and unwritten. Company policies could be in contravention of legislation that governs the employment relationship.

Whether you are on the verge of expansion or trying to improve employment practices, you will find the information you need in this book, *From Entrepreneur to Employer*.

Building a strong team of employees involves, among other things, hiring the right people, making sound decisions on pay and benefits, complying with legislation, and managing staff effectively. Whether you are forming or rebuilding a team, you can find everything you need to know on-line. But knowing what to look for can be challenging. As the saying goes, "You don't know what you don't know."

That is why, after more than 30 years as a human resources practitioner and manager, I established a freelance consultancy designed for small business owners. My clients, both new and evolving enterprises, required help with policies and procedures, legislative compliance, hiring and firing, job descriptions, performance management, employee discipline, conflict resolution, and team building. Occasionally, they just needed a sounding board or general advice.

As I was unable to find a comprehensive source of suitable reference material for my clients, I decided to write this book. In *From Entrepreneur to Employer* you will learn how to comply with employment legislation, find the right staff, administer pay, select a benefits plan, manage people, and more.

The Legal Environment (Chapter 1) is particularly important because legislation governs so many of your decisions about employment practices. Furthermore, as statutes are subject to change, you will need to know how to find the most current information. This chapter gives you an overview of important legislation and where to find it.

At the end of the book is a list of resources such as government websites wherein you can find current legislation and other useful facts.

Also provided is a glossary of terms. Using the right terminology can facilitate on-line searches.

I have arranged the book in a logical order, but the information is interrelated. Yes, it makes sense for you to create an employee manual early on (Chapter 2), but you cannot do it without reference to other sections of this guide. While finding the right employees (Chapter 3) precedes preparing for the new employee (Chapter 4), these activities can be undertaken concurrently. You will know what works best for you.

The material presented herein is introductory and dependent on my experience. Once you have established the basics, further study may be helpful. Chapter 8, for example, introduces human resources (HR) management. You will benefit from reading works by many highly qualified experts who have written extensively on this subject.

This book is written for employers in Ontario, but may be helpful in other jurisdictions, subject to differences in legislation. Each province and territory has similar laws which can be found on-line.

I wish you every success in your journey from entrepreneur to employer.

Pam

CHAPTER 1

The Legal Environment

You and your employees have legal rights and responsibilities, so you will want to ensure that your policies, practices, and procedures comply with the law.

The federal and provincial governments have statutory (i.e., written) laws that affect the way you interact with employees. The Government of Canada administers tax laws for most provinces and territories and manages national programs like the Canada Pension Plan (CPP) and Employment Insurance (EI). It also regulates certain industries and workplaces through the *Canada Labour Code* (CLC). A list of federally regulated industries and workplaces is provided at the end of this chapter.

Companies not subject to the CLC are provincially or territorially regulated and must comply with the statutes of the provinces and territories where they do business. Provincial and territorial laws cover topics such as employment standards, human rights, pay equity, accessibility, and privacy.

In addition, common law (case law) governs the contractual relationship between an employer and an employee. This body of unwritten laws, which is based on legal precedents established by the courts, applies in all jurisdictions except Quebec. That province is governed by the *Quebec Civil Code*.

The focus of this book is on businesses regulated by the Province of Ontario. Chapter 1 introduces the government bodies responsible for various legislation and provides an overview of laws that affect the employment relationship in Ontario.

Ontario's Ministry of Labour, Training and Skills Development

In Ontario, the Ministry of Labour, Training and Skills Development is responsible for employment matters. It administers employment standards, workplace health and safety, pay equity, and labour relations legislation. This ministry also provides information and services for employers and job seekers.

Employment Standards

The *Employment Standards Act, 2000* defines the minimum standards of work for employees. Each province and territory has its own legislation, which is similar, but not identical, to that of Ontario.

Standards include, for example
> ➤ hours of work and overtime pay.
> ➤ statutory holidays and public holiday pay.

> vacations and vacation pay.
> minimum wages.
> equal pay for equal work.
> legislated leaves of absence.
> minimum notice and severance pay when terminating employment without just cause.
> how long specific records must be maintained.

Understanding your employment standards obligations is important because running afoul of legislation can be costly. The Ministry of Labour, Training and Skills Development conducts annual audit inspections to ensure compliance with employment standards and safety legislation, and to educate employers and employees about their rights and responsibilities. Ministry inspectors have the authority to issue compliance orders requiring a company to correct any issues within a given time. They can also issue notices of contravention, fines, and in extreme cases, jail time. In addition, employers will have to cover the cost of compliance, such as retroactive overtime pay should an audit uncover the employer's failure to make appropriate payment of wages.

To stay informed, you can check the website of the Ministry of Labour, Training and Skills Development. There, you will find details of annual inspection blitzes that identify the focus, program, sector/business type, and scheduled dates. The website also reports the results of past inspections, including the names of those companies convicted of an offence.

Occupational Health and Safety

Employers in Ontario are responsible for protecting the health and safety of their employees at work. The *Occupational Health and Safety Act* requires employers to maintain a safe workplace, provide the necessary training (including first aid), keep records of training completed by each person, maintain safety equipment and clothing, appoint competent supervisors, and develop a health and safety policy, as well as policies with respect to workplace violence and workplace harassment. Details are available on the website of the Ministry of Labour, Training and Skills Development.

Currently, most workplaces with 6 to 19 workers are required to have a health and safety representative, and those with 20 or more must have a joint health and safety committee.

Workers have the right to be involved in ensuring a safe workplace and the right to refuse unsafe work.

The legislation also requires that the following be displayed in the workplace:

➤ A copy of the *Occupational Health and Safety Act*
➤ A copy of the poster, Health and Safety at Work: Prevention Starts Here
➤ A copy of a written occupational health and safety policy developed and maintained by the company

➤ For employers with more than five employees, copies of the company's workplace violence and workplace harassment policies

If a person is critically injured or killed in the workplace, you must notify the ministry's Health and Safety Contact Centre, the health and safety representative or joint health and safety committee, and the union, if there is one. You should also contact a lawyer experienced in workplace incidents.

The ministry will immediately dispatch an investigator who has the authority to lay charges. You and your employees need to know your rights. During an investigation interview, an employee may inadvertently make a statement that incriminates your business or an individual in your organization.

Workplace Hazardous Materials Information System

The Workplace Hazardous Materials Information System (WHMIS) is Canada's national hazard communication standard. Its purpose is to ensure that workers receive hazard information about materials that are used at their work sites to reduce workplace injuries. In Ontario, this standard is administered by the Ministry of Labour, Training and Skills Development.

WHMIS requires employers to

> ➤ educate and train workers on the hazards and safe use of hazardous products in the workplace.
> ➤ ensure that hazardous products are properly labelled.
> ➤ prepare workplace labels and safety data sheets (as necessary).
> ➤ ensure appropriate control measures are in place to protect the health and safety of workers.

WHMIS requires workers to

> ➤ participate in WHMIS and chemical safety training programs.
> ➤ take necessary steps to protect themselves and their co-workers.
> ➤ participate in identifying and controlling hazards.

Information about WHMIS can be found on the ministry's website.

Labour Relations (Unions)

If you have unionized employees, your policies, practices, and procedures will be governed by the *Labour Relations Act, 1995* instead of the *Employment Standards Act, 2000*.

Common law generally does not apply in a unionized environment because collective agreements cover all aspects of the employment relationship.

For further information, see Unions (Chapter 9).

Ontario Human Rights Commission

As an employer you are required to comply with human rights legislation and to have in place fair and equitable policies and practices to prohibit discrimination and harassment. The Ontario Human Rights Commission, an arm's length agency of the provincial government, establishes and enforces human rights legislation through the *Ontario Human Rights Code* (Code) and the Human Rights Tribunal of Ontario.

Ontario Human Rights Code

The Code prohibits discrimination and harassment in employment on the basis of age, ancestry, colour, race, citizenship, ethnic origin, place of origin, creed, disability (including sick leave and addiction), family status, marital status (including single status), gender identity, gender expression, record of offences, sex (including pregnancy and breastfeeding), and sexual orientation. These are referred to as the prohibited grounds of discrimination.

Discrimination can be direct or systemic. Systemic discrimination occurs when a rule or requirement that seems to be fair to everyone inadvertently excludes someone in a designated group. For example, requiring a prospective employee to have Canadian experience discriminates against people new to Canada.

In certain circumstances, where there is a *bona fide occupational requirement (BFOR)*, the Code permits an

7

employer to implement a requirement or qualification that could result in discrimination on the basis of one of the prohibited grounds. To establish that a requirement or qualification is a BFOR, the employer must meet a three-part test:

- ➤ The employer must have adopted the requirement or qualification for a purpose that is rationally connected to the performance of the job.

- ➤ The employer must have adopted the requirement or qualification in an honest and good faith belief that it was necessary to the fulfillment of that legitimate work-related purpose.

- ➤ The requirement or qualification must be reasonably necessary to accomplish that legitimate work-related purpose. To show that the standard is reasonably necessary, it must be demonstrated that it is impossible to accommodate individual employees sharing the characteristics of the claimant without imposing undue hardship upon the employer.

As an example, the need for a construction worker to be able to lift and carry a certain weight may be a BFOR.

Employers have a duty to accommodate the needs of employees to the point of undue hardship to the employer. Such accommodations might include providing special equipment to allow those with disabilities to perform their duties, or rearranging shifts to allow employees to celebrate religious holidays.

Funding for special equipment may be available through the Ontario Disability Support Program which is managed by the Ministry of Children, Community and Social Services.

When administering drug or alcohol tests, employers must be able to prove that the tests are BFORs because an addiction to alcohol or drugs may be considered a disability under the Code. Ontario's *Human Rights Code* policy on drug and alcohol testing states that testing may be *prima facie* discriminatory (accepted as discriminatory unless proven otherwise).

Even when confident that it has met the conditions for a BFOR, an employer should proceed with caution. For example, a test may be conducted only after an offer of employment has been made. If a candidate is recognized as having a drug or alcohol dependency, the employer must treat this as a disability and offer reasonable accommodation to the individual. This might include referral to an employee assistance program.

In Ontario, random drug testing is seen as justifiable in limited situations. The employer must demonstrate that an employee's impairment represents an unacceptable risk, such as in safety-sensitive positions.

Employees' right to privacy trumps an employer's right to test unless there is either clear and unequivocal contractual or statutory consent or reasonable cause to allow random drug testing.

Human Rights Tribunal of Ontario

An employee who believes that they have been discriminated against or harassed based on one of the prohibited grounds may file a human rights complaint with the Human Rights Tribunal of Ontario (HRTO). The HRTO attempts to resolve issues through mediation before holding a hearing. If there is a hearing, and the employer is found to have discriminated against the employee on one or more prohibited grounds, they may be ordered to provide monetary compensation as well as to take whatever action is necessary to promote future compliance with the Code.

If the employee has been fired based on a prohibited ground, the HRTO has the authority to order that they be reinstated.

Ontario Pay Equity Commission

The Ontario Pay Equity Commission (Commission) is responsible for promoting gender economic equality by administering the province's *Pay Equity Act* (Act).

Under the Act, employers who have had 10 or more employees at any time after December 31, 1987, must achieve pay equity within their workforce. The Act is based on the assumption that work performed by women has been traditionally underpaid due to systemic gender discrimination, and its goal is to redress gender discrimination in the compensation or pay of employees in female job classes.

Pay equity goes beyond *equal pay for equal work* and requires *equal pay for work of equal value*. This means employers need to evaluate the work of job classes held primarily by females, and those held predominantly by males, on the basis of skill, effort, responsibility, and working conditions. Through such comparison an organization might determine, for example, that the jobs of receptionist and shipper/receiver are of equal value.

If a male-dominated job pays more than a female-dominated job of the same value, the company must raise the salaries of those in the female-dominated job to at least the same level. Men working in the female-dominated job are to receive the same increases as their female colleagues.

The method of comparing jobs is left to the employer. Several companies offer job-evaluation methods, and the Commission has guides and e-tools for comparing jobs and preparing your own pay equity plan.

If you are subject to the *Pay Equity Act*, the Commission may include you in its annual targeted review of employer groups, which includes new employers. To prepare for this possibility, you will want to read the information on the Commission's website. Summaries of review findings are available from the Commission upon request.

The Accessibility Directorate of Ontario

In Ontario, every organization or business is required to develop, implement, and maintain policies governing how they create accessibility, or will create it, for people with disabilities. The *Accessibility for Ontarians with Disabilities Act, 2005* (AODA) is the law that protects and enforces accessibility rights. The Accessibility Directorate of Ontario helps implement the legislation by advising the Minister in Charge of the AODA.

The AODA requires organizations and businesses to meet standards in five areas: customer service, employment, information and communication, transportation, and design of public spaces.

The Customer Service Standard requires that all employers who provide goods and services to members of the public, and who have 50 or more employees, create and document customer service policies. These policies are to be made publicly available in an accessible format. The employers must also train their staff on accessible customer service and on how to interact with people with different disabilities. The employer must keep a log of all training completed.

The Employment Standard requires all employers to notify their employees and the public about the availability of accommodation for applicants with disabilities in their recruitment processes. They must inform employees of company policies on the provision of job accommodations to assist employees with disabilities.

The Information and Communication Standard requires all employers to make their emergency procedures, public safety information, feedback processes, and information accessible to people with disabilities on request.

The Transportation Standard applies to organizations providing public transportation services. It requires the provider to make information available on accessibility equipment and features of their vehicles, routes, and services.

The Design of Public Spaces Standard requires companies with fifty or more employees to make spaces accessible to people with disabilities when building or renovating outdoor eating areas, play spaces, trails, and so on.

While these requirements may sound daunting, they do not have to be. For example, making printed information available for customers with a visual impairment may be as simple as reading it to them.

The Ontario government lists guides and resources on its accessibility website.

Federal Contractors' Program (Employment Equity)

While provincially regulated businesses are not covered by the federal *Employment Equity Act*, they may be covered by the Federal Contractors' Program which is managed by Employment and Social Development Canada. Organizations with 100 or more employees that want to bid on a federal government contract or a standing offer of $1 million or more must first sign an Agreement to Implement Employment Equity. The organization is assigned an *Agreement to Implement Employment Equity Number*, to be reported on each bid submitted.

The Federal Contractors' Program requires employers to conduct a workforce analysis and to develop plans to improve their hiring, retention, and promotion of people from four designated groups that have been traditionally under-represented in the workforce. These include women, aboriginal peoples, members of visible minorities, and persons with disabilities.

Details of the program are available from Employment and Social Development Canada.

Privacy

Employees are entitled to have their private and personal information protected, and both the federal and provincial governments take this seriously. Departments and agencies at both levels of government are required to protect private information. In addition, certain legislation dictates the measures employers must put in place to protect personal information they collect.

Canada Revenue Agency

The Canada Revenue Agency (CRA) requires employers to keep employee information, including electronic data, in a secure place or in encrypted computer files. Only authorized company representatives may have access to these files and only to information needed for their job. For example, a payroll administrator may access payroll information, but not other confidential employee information.

Personal Information Protection and Electronic Documents Act (PIPEDA)

The federal *Personal Information Protection and Electronic Documents Act* (PIPEDA) applies to private sector organizations engaged in commercial activity in Ontario. Most not-for-profit and charity groups will not be subject to PIPEDA. The legislation is designed to protect personal information that is collected, used, or disclosed in certain circumstances. PIPEDA states that an organization is responsible for the personal information under its control; the purpose for which the personal information is collected should be identified before or at the time it is collected; and the knowledge and consent of the individual must be obtained before personal information is collected, used, or disclosed.

PIPEDA may also apply to employee information collected by an employer, such as age, marital status, employment history and social insurance number. Personal information does not include the name, title, business address, or business telephone number of an employee of an organization.

To meet the basic requirements of PIPEDA employers must

> ➤ obtain the clear consent of an individual before they collect, use, or disclose personal information about that individual.

> ➤ only use the information collected for the purposes for which they have consent.

> ➤ protect information from unauthorized access and use.

> ➤ keep information up to date and correctly filed so that decisions are based on correct information.

> ➤ destroy information when they no longer need it for the original purpose.

> ➤ implement accountability mechanisms in their organizations to ensure compliance with the above (including appointing a compliance officer).

This privacy legislation would also apply to sales representatives' client contact information.

Personal Health Information Protection Act, 2004

Ontario's *Personal Health Information Protection Act, 2004* is intended for health care custodians, such as hospitals, but if an employer receives personal health information from a custodian they may "only use or disclose the information for the authorized purpose for which it was disclosed or for the purpose of carrying out a statutory or legal duty."

Employers may have to obtain information, such as health benefits claims and substance monitoring reports, which could be considered private health information. To respect the spirit of the law, I would keep only what is necessary, and store any data related to personal health separately from an employee's general file.

Federally Regulated Businesses

As noted in the introduction to this chapter, some companies are federally regulated. If your business falls into one of the following categories, you are covered by the CLC, so this book does not apply to you:

➢ Banks
➢ Marine shipping, ferry, and port services
➢ Air transportation, including airports, aerodromes, and airlines
➢ Railway and road transportation that involves crossing provincial or international borders

- ➤ Canals, pipelines, tunnels, and bridges (crossing provincial borders)
- ➤ Telephone, telegraph, and cable systems
- ➤ Radio and television broadcasting
- ➤ Grain elevators, feed and seed mills
- ➤ Uranium mining and processing
- ➤ Businesses dealing with the protection of fisheries as a natural resource
- ➤ Many First Nation activities
- ➤ Most federal Crown corporations
- ➤ Private businesses necessary to the operation of a federal act

For further information, refer to the Federal Labour Standards on the Government of Canada website.

Common Law

Employment standards legislation defines minimum requirements for dealing with employees. As a contract between an employer and an employee, an employment relationship may also be subject to the common law, which is a body of law (or principles) derived from judicial decisions of the courts in Ontario.

Common law is more complicated than written law, and often requires the aid of a lawyer to interpret. This book cannot adequately cover such a complex topic, but the following section identifies some areas to note.

As mentioned, under common law an employment relationship is a contract between the employer and the employee. A contract involves an offer, an acceptance, and consideration (i.e., a benefit that is bargained for between the parties). In employment, the employer receives the employee's labour in return for pay and other benefits. If the employer wishes to make fundamental changes to the contract of employment after the employee is hired, further consideration (such as an increase in pay) must be offered by the employer and accepted by the employee. The same would be true if an employee wished to make fundamental changes, but typically the employer has the advantage in negotiations.

Common law becomes an issue when an employer unilaterally changes an employee's conditions of employment (e.g., transfer or demotion) or terminates employment without just cause.

The first situation is referred to as constructive dismissal. By changing the terms of the original contract without the employee's agreement, without consideration, or without reasonable notice, the employer has effectively fired the employee. As a result, the employee can resign and sue for damages. These damages might be restricted to the requirements of the employment standards legislation to give notice (if the contract of employment clearly limits an employee's entitlements) or be based on common law principles of reasonable notice.

With some exceptions (e.g., those covered by human rights legislation) an employer can terminate someone's employment contract for any reason. However, in the absence of just cause for dismissal, the employer must provide reasonable notice or compensation in lieu of notice. If there is no clear, well-understood agreement as to what constitutes reasonable notice (i.e., did the employee agree in the contract that the minimums provided by the employment standards legislation would be sufficient), a court will decide the appropriate length of notice to be granted. The court's decision will be based on factors such as the employee's age, length of service, position, and salary, and the availability of similar employment. It will also be based on precedents set by recent court cases. Reasonable notice, as defined at common law, can be significantly longer than the minimums established by employment standards legislation.

Accordingly, even if an employer complies with the legislation by providing an employee with the required minimum notice or pay in lieu of notice, it may have to provide additional compensation to account for common law reasonable notice. If the court determines that the employer's conduct during the termination was designed to humiliate, degrade, and/or harass an employee, it may also order an additional amount be paid in punitive damages.

Employees who have been terminated without cause are expected to mitigate their potential damages by seeking suitable new employment. Any compensation ordered by a court will be reduced by the amount earned at the new job during the notice period. This is sometimes seen as a disincentive for employees to start their job search. As a result, some employers structure their termination packages such that they will pay half of the remaining agreed-upon salary continuance payment as a lump sum if the employee finds another job.

Just cause for termination of employment includes wilful misconduct, disobedience, wilful neglect of duty, insubordination, or theft. This type of behaviour must not have been condoned by the employer. It seems straightforward, but there is a wealth of case law in which people terminated for cause have successfully sued for damages.

Unless it is a specific term of the employee's contract of employment with your company, laying off an employee, even for a short period, will be considered a constructive dismissal. In such a case, the employee will be able to seek notice as a result of the termination (i.e., to resign and sue the employer for notice based on the employment standards legislation minimums or common law).

The principles of common law notice apply only in the courts. At the time of termination, some employers will offer only the minimum notice required under employment standards legislation, hoping that the employee will not take them to court or pursue a claim through a lawyer. However, if there is no contract limiting the employee's entitlement to the employment standards minimums, employers should be prepared to settle for a higher amount of notice if necessary.

CHAPTER 2

Getting Started

A successful business expansion will require hiring the right people, in the right positions, for the right compensation. To determine what this means for your company, you will want to develop a plan that identifies the type of workforce you need and the terms of employment.

Define the Work to be Done

Start planning by defining the work to be done. Even if it seems clear that you need help with sales, marketing, administration, or production, take time to conduct a detailed analysis.

Make a list of everything you need to accomplish and identify the work you want to delegate. Then write job descriptions; one for yourself, with the responsibilities you will keep, and one (or more) for the work to be delegated. This will define the roles your company will need in its expansion.

Before you start writing a job description, conduct a job analysis, which is a process of collecting and recording all the details of a job. Ask yourself the following:

➤ What are the most important tasks and projects required of the job?

➤ What necessary education, knowledge, skills, and personal attributes will be required of candidates? Personal attributes are qualities like creativity, resourcefulness, flexibility, integrity, communication skills, organizational skills, decision-making skills, being a team player, and so on.

➤ What skills must candidates bring to the table and which can be easily taught?

➤ What is the work environment like and who would thrive in it? For example, will your staff work in a busy, open atmosphere or in a quiet, enclosed space? Is there potential of exposure to excessive noise, dangerous products, or stressful situations?

➤ Are there any unique requirements, such as shift work, regular overtime, and travel?

➤ Are there bona fide occupational requirements (as per Ontario's *Human Rights Code*), and what accommodations can be made, if required, to help the person fit the job?

➤ To which position will the job report, and which positions, if any, will report to this job?

➤ How will you monitor an employee's progress and deliver feedback and coaching?

Incorporate the information gathered into a job description. Begin with the job title, and a summary of the purpose of the job. The purpose of a sales representative might be *to promote and sell ABC Company products in an assigned territory.* Add as much information as is necessary to define the job. For example

> ➢ A summary of the duties and responsibilities of the job
> ➢ Qualifications required including education, skills, and personal attributes
> ➢ Reporting relationships
> ➢ Working conditions
> ➢ Unique requirements

If you need help, you can find guidelines and examples of job descriptions on-line. Search for *how to write a job description.* You can also find useful information in the National Occupational Classification (NOC) maintained by Employment and Social Development Canada. For each classification, the NOC lists sample job titles, main duties, employment requirements, and relevant additional information. The U.S. Department of Labor's O*Net system is another source. It may present additional job detail.

Determine the Type of Employees You Require

Companies can have a mix of full-time, part-time, and temporary employees. Your budget and the work to be done will help you to decide what type of employment to offer.

A **full-time** position usually requires a person to work 30 to 40 hours per week, as defined by an employment contract or company policy. Full-time employees are usually entitled to all benefits offered by the business, as well as legislated benefits.

A **part-time** position generally requires someone to work less than 30 hours per week, as defined by an employment contract or company policy. Part-time employees may or may not be entitled to employer-sponsored benefits but are entitled to all legislated benefits.

A **temporary** position can be full-time or part-time. The worker is hired for a specific length of time, or for a specific task. While not usually entitled to employer-sponsored benefits, temporary employees are entitled to legislated benefits. Many organizations use employment agencies to supply staff in this category. This means the individual is an employee of the agency, which is responsible for paying the employee, providing benefits, and replacing an unsatisfactory candidate. The agency's billing rate will be higher than what you would pay the worker, but hiring this way is sometimes worthwhile for the convenience of having someone else deal with details.

Independent contractors are not employees, but I include them in this list because some employers mistakenly confuse them with dependent contractors. An independent contractor is someone who has their own business, has full control over their own work, and has other clients. You compensate them by paying the invoices they send you for work completed and any eligible expenses, plus applicable sales tax. It is important to have a written contract that outlines all expectations. This will make it clear to the CRA that this person is not an employee and will reduce the risk of misunderstandings and billing disputes. The CRA provides guidelines to determine whether an individual is considered an employee or an independent contractor. You have a business-to-business relationship with an independent contractor.

Dependent contractor is a term used to recognize individuals whose employment, although involving some degree of independence, involves a degree of economic dependence on the company when viewed in the totality of economic activity. The relationship is more that of an employee than of a self-employed person or independent contractor. If a worker is deemed to be a dependent contractor, they are entitled to regular employee legislated benefits and protections. A dependent contractor is economically dependent on a specific client.

A **remote worker** (also known as homeworker) is an employee who works for you from their home or other location. The *Employment Standards Act, 2000* includes guidelines for employing homeworkers, and most legislation that applies to workers on your premises applies to them. This can create special challenges in, for example, monitoring for compliance with employment standards, ensuring a safe work environment, or protecting confidential company and client data. Remote workers are entitled to income tax deductions for expenses paid for the workspace in their homes if you provide them with Form 2200 Declaration of Conditions of Employment. Remote employees should be made aware that when their residence is sold, any expenses claimed while working at home may trigger a capital gains tax on the portion of the house used for business purposes.

Decide How Employees Will Be Paid

In Ontario, employees may be paid by cash, cheque, or direct deposit into their account at a bank or other type of financial institution. If payment is by cash or cheque, the employee must be paid the wages at the workplace or at some other place agreed to, electronically or in writing, by the employee.

Hourly employees are paid only for the time worked and may be full-time, part-time, or temporary workers. They are usually required to record their hours by completing timesheets or punching a time clock.

Salaried employees are paid not for hours worked, but for the work accomplished during a set daily, weekly, or monthly schedule. They are paid based on a weekly, monthly, or annual rate and are not required to record their hours.

Typically, managerial and professional employees are paid a salary.

Exception-hourly employees (a category used by some payroll companies) work the same hours each week and are automatically paid for their regular hours. Adjustments for events like sick days or overtime are made on the first pay following the exceptional event.

Many employers think that salaried employees do not have to be paid for overtime work. However, under provincial employment standards legislation, certain jobs are exempt from overtime pay, while all others are not exempt.

In the case of managers and supervisors in Ontario, if their job regularly requires them to perform work that is not exempt from overtime pay, they are entitled to be paid for their overtime hours for the non-exempt work.

Determine Your Budget

To manage your employment expenses, you will want to calculate the actual costs of having employees. Each time you hire someone, you establish an ongoing commitment, which involves more than simply paying them a wage or salary. You will need to factor in all the costs of employing workers. For example

> Salary and related costs
> - Base pay
> - Commission or bonus, if applicable

- ○ CPP and EI contributions
- ○ Workplace Safety and Insurance Board (WSIB) premiums
- ○ Vacation pay and holiday pay
- ○ Benefits premiums, if applicable
- ○ Termination and severance pay obligations
- ○ Payroll processing costs if you use a payroll company or your accountant

➢ Other costs
- ○ Additional workspace, if needed
- ○ Office equipment and supplies (e.g., desks, chairs, filing cabinets, stationery, IT hardware, software, and licences)
- ○ Tools
- ○ Additional liability and errors and omissions insurance, if appropriate
- ○ Reimbursable expenses (e.g., gas, mileage, parking, and meals)
- ○ Other expenses specific to your situation

Define Your Business

When you decided to start a business, you had a vision for a product or service that you wanted to sell, and probably had a business plan. As an employer you will have certain expectations of your employees and a concept of how to treat customers. However, the people you hire will not know your intentions unless you put the information in writing for circulation to your staff.

Businesses often use written statements that outline their mission, vision, and values to provide clarity for their employees and clients.

A mission statement describes what you want to accomplish or the raison d'être of the business; a vision statement establishes where you want to be in the future; values define your beliefs and how you expect staff to behave. For example,

Puma's mission is "To be the Fastest Sports Brand in the World."

The vision of the Alzheimer's Association is "A World Without Alzheimer's Disease."

Facebook's values are "Focus on impact, Move fast, Be bold, Be open, Build social value".

If you can define what you want to accomplish, your vision of the future, and how you expect employees to behave, your staff will know how to align themselves with your business goals.

Create an Employee Handbook

As you think about building your business, you will want to consider the implications of employing people. You will need to comply with legislation, establish policies and procedures, and define any benefits you wish to offer. The discipline of writing an employee handbook will help you to organize your thoughts and develop an HR strategy.

Benefits of a Handbook

An employee handbook (also referred to as an employee manual or a policy manual) is a document that serves as a rulebook and reference guide for the workplace. It outlines your expectations of employees and what they can expect from you. It also provides clarity and reduces misunderstanding of company policies, practices, and procedures.

A handbook that has been read and acknowledged by all employees becomes part of the employment contract. If you communicate policies and consistently apply them, you will be able to rely on the terms of these policies to discipline or terminate employees. For this reason, it is best to have your handbook reviewed, or written, by an employment lawyer.

Typical Content

You might begin with a letter of welcome, an introduction to your business and, if you have them, your mission, vision, and values.

I have commented below on some of the more common items found in employee handbooks. You can also find samples and templates on-line. Your own situation will dictate what to include, and what to exclude.

Expectations: What do you expect of employees, and what can they expect of you?

Hours of work: When will the workday begin and end, and how many breaks (paid or unpaid) will employees be entitled to take? Will the day be structured, with set start and end times, or will it be more flexible? Whatever form the workday takes, it must comply with employment standards legislation. After they work five hours, employees are entitled to a 30-minute unpaid period in which to eat. There are limits on the number of hours you can require employees to work in a week unless more hours are agreed to in writing. For most employees, the limits are eight hours in a regular workday, and forty-eight hours in a week.

Method of pay: How and when will people be paid? Hourly employees are paid only for the actual hours worked. Salaried employees are paid for a specific period. For example, a salaried employee may be paid an agreed amount per week, month, or year. Typical pay periods can be weekly (52 pays per year), bi-weekly (26 pays per year), or monthly (12 pays per year).

Deductions from pay: It is useful, especially for young employees, to outline what the company will be deducting from each pay. Typical deductions include income tax, CPP and EI contributions, and premiums for insured benefits.

Overtime pay: Who is eligible for overtime pay, and how is it structured and administered? Are employees allowed to bank overtime hours and take them as time off in lieu (1.5 hours is to be banked for each hour worked), or do overtime hours have to be paid out when earned? Does your policy comply with employment standards legislation?

Shift differentials: If individuals are required to work outside the regular workday, (e.g., night shift), will they be given additional compensation? What are the details? While not required, paying shift differentials may be helpful in recruiting for these hard-to-fill positions.

On-call and call-in pay: If you have employees who will be on call (i.e., not at work but available to be called in at a moment's notice) or who are called in but work less than three hours, the *Employment Standards Act, 2000* requires that they receive three hours' pay.

Performance reviews and salary reviews: How, and how often, will you review employee performance? How will you make salary decisions and how often? Will salary increases be tied to performance reviews? If not, what criteria will be used to decide salary increases? (See Chapter 8)

Vacation and vacation pay: Will you have a common vacation entitlement date (e.g., based on the calendar year), or will employees' entitlements be based on their hire dates? Are there any times during the year when employees cannot schedule vacation? Will you offer vacation time over and above the statutory minimum requirement, and if so, how will extra time be earned?

Will vacation pay be paid as earned (i.e., on each pay day), or when vacation time is taken? How will you ensure the amount paid is equal to the amount earned (4% of annual gross earnings for two weeks' vacation, 6% for three weeks, and so on)? Do your policies comply with employment standards legislation?

Employee benefits (see Chapter 7): What, if any, benefits do you offer and how are they administered? How do employees register for and find more information about their benefits? Do employees pay for their benefits? If they do, include information on when premium rates are reviewed and may be increased (usually annually). How can the employer modify the benefits offered? Your benefits provider or consultant can ensure that your plans have clear language authorizing amendments. Include this information in your handbook.

Leaves of absence: The Ontario government mandates job-protected leaves of absence in certain situations. Most people are aware of the requirement to grant pregnancy and parental leave, but, as of this writing, at least 10 other situations may require an employer to allow time off. Details are available on the website of the Ministry of Labour, Training and Skills Development. In most cases, you do not have to pay employees while they are on government-mandated leave, but you might want to help relieve their financial burden during stressful events. In addition, how will you deal with other absences such as extended illness and jury duty?

Standards of behaviour: What are your expectations of employee behaviour and what are the consequences if an employee does not meet the standards? Will you create a set process to manage expectations? Do your rules and processes comply with legislation?

Confidentiality and privacy: You may wish to have a policy that spells out the employees' responsibility to keep company and client information confidential, or require employees to sign a confidentiality agreement. This is such a critical issue that some companies specify that a breach of privacy will be considered just cause for dismissal without notice.

Use of company electronic devices: Today, almost every employee has access to a company computer and, according to one survey, 64 percent of employees visit non-work-related sites every day at work. In setting policies, you need to consider personal use and related risks.

You may decide not to allow any personal use of business-owned electronic devices. Otherwise, a well-defined policy can protect against the risks involved. Such a policy might stipulate that the electronic devices are the sole property of the business and that employees should have no expectation of privacy when using them. Bear in mind, however, that the Supreme Court of Canada has indicated (*R.v.Cole*) that "even where an electronic device is issued and ultimately owned by an employer, an employee may have a reasonable expectation of privacy in that device so long as some incidental personal use is permitted."

Policies on the use of company electronic devices usually include guidelines for appropriate usage, computer etiquette, downloading of software, changing and protecting passwords, and prohibited sites on the internet.

Policies prohibiting discrimination and harassment: Discrimination or harassment at work may create a poisoned work environment. It can also lead to an employee filing a claim that the employer and/or a fellow employee have violated the provincial *Human Rights Code*. Your company should have a policy which explains what the applicable terms mean, provides a means for employees to report or make complaints, assures them that complaints will be dealt with fairly, and spells out the penalties for abusers. A workplace violence and harassment policy is mandatory in Ontario for employers with more than five employees.

Health and safety: As noted in Chapter 1, employers must comply with Ontario's *Occupational Health and Safety Act*. Explain where employees can find copies of your occupational health and safety policy, copies of the health and safety act and poster, and information about required personal protective equipment. Provide information on who is trained in first aid, how to report an accident and whether the company has a trained health and safety representative. Include the procedure for refusing unsafe work, and particulars of employees' rights and responsibilities in the event of an incident inspection by the Ministry of Health.

Dress code: Do you need a dress code? If so, describe how employees are expected to dress and how the rules will be enforced. (see Chapter 9).

Temporary layoff: Will you reserve the right to lay off staff under certain circumstances? If so, provide details. As noted under Common Law (Chapter 1), you normally need an enforceable written contract that allows you to do this.

Making changes: Include a statement that the employer reserves the right to change policies and procedures, and thus the contents of the handbook, at any time, with or without notice.

I strongly recommend obtaining legal advice before implementing a handbook. An employment lawyer can review it for you, or write it, to ensure compliance with legislation and to protect your business.

As an employee handbook may be considered contractual in nature, the information needs to be current. Review your handbook at least annually to revise policies if necessary and to ensure compliance with changes to legislation.

CHAPTER 3

Recruiting:
Finding The Right Employees

One of your most important responsibilities as an employer is finding and retaining the right people. Finding the person who is a good fit will contribute to business success, while hiring the wrong person can be costly.

Recruiting can be challenging. A candidate may have the education and training, but not the necessary personal attributes. Some people are good at presenting themselves in interviews but may not be as qualified as less polished applicants. Interviewers may have personal biases that prevent them from recognizing the qualities of good candidates. You can improve your chances of hiring the right person by using the following approach.

Define Your Needs

Start the recruiting process by reviewing and updating the job description for the open position. Ensure that you have a good understanding of the job responsibilities as well as the qualifications, skills, and attributes of the person you want to hire.

Write Your Recruitment Advertisement

A recruitment advertisement usually includes information about the company, where the job is located, a job title and responsibilities, the qualifications required of candidates, and how to apply for the position. Use your job description as a guide. The more accurately you define your requirements, the easier it will be for job seekers to judge if they will be a good fit. Some companies include salary information while others prefer to keep salary confidential.

If you need inspiration, look at similar jobs posted on recruitment sites.

Identify Your Potential Talent Pool

To focus your search, you will want to identify where you are most likely to find good candidates and how you will reach them.

If you do not have the time to devote to recruiting or wish to keep the name of your business confidential, consider hiring a professional employment agent. They have the experience, keep up to date on the latest recruiting tools, sometimes have qualified jobseekers already available, and in most cases, charge you only if you hire one of their candidates.

Most agencies also offer a replacement guarantee, but if you choose wisely and give them enough information about the job and your expectations, they should get it right the first time.

If you decide to work with recruiters, make sure that they have the right knowledge and experience. Interview them, ask for references, find out how many similar positions they have filled and how often they have had to honour their guarantee because a candidate was not the right fit.

Generally, I would hire a recruiter on contingency, which means that you would not pay them unless you hire one of their applicants. However, for more difficult assignments, such as finding specialized candidates who are in high demand, it is sometimes worth hiring an experienced agent on consignment, which means paying them to conduct a search on your behalf.

If you decide to do your own recruiting, you can reach candidates through various sources.

Many people are using social media to search for jobs. Establishing a presence on the most popular sites may help to attract candidates. LinkedIn, for example, which is designed for business, includes recruiting tools and a job posting service.

Internet-based job boards such as Workopolis, Monster, ZipRecruiter, and Indeed will publish your job ads and provide recruiting tools to assist in your search.

University or college on-line job boards offer a quick way to reach recent graduates with specific educational backgrounds. Graduates with more experience may also check these boards.

Trade publications advertise relevant job opportunities, but because they tend to publish monthly or quarterly, they may not be timely enough for your needs.

The Government of Canada website includes a job bank where you can post open positions at no cost. This website also provides business and industry information you would find useful as an employer.

Veterans Affairs Canada offers a free job bank marketed to veterans, and advises:

> Canada's military men and women are known around the world for their leadership skills, teamwork, and dedication. They are highly skilled in areas such as planning, communication, management, and the trades. Without question, they would be an asset to any workforce.

Employment and Social Development Canada has a website with information about hiring persons with disabilities. The site includes a link to the Discover Ability Network, which puts employers in touch with candidates.

Referrals from existing employees can be helpful. They may have friends or acquaintances who would be a good fit. Some companies offer employees a referral bonus, payable when the candidate is hired or has passed probation. My preference is to pay the bonus when the person is hired because the employee's only role is to refer a suitable candidate. The responsibility of hiring the right person rests with the manager.

Trade apprentices can be hired through the Ontario Youth Apprenticeship Program. The focus of this program is to train young people and to provide employers with the opportunity to develop the skilled workers they require.

Newspapers still run printed advertisements and may provide the option of on-line posting as well as running the print ad.

Collect and Screen Applications

After determining how to advertise a job opening, you will need to decide how to process applications. The internet, for example, reaches many people, but can also attract a high volume of responses, often from people who are not qualified. Some recruiters set an application deadline to limit the number of responses or to expedite the hiring process.

Decide how you want people to apply for the job. If you use social media and on-line job boards, you can have candidates upload a résumé or complete an electronic application form. If people are to apply by e-mail, you may wish to set up a designated e-mail account.

Otherwise, your inbox may be inundated with responses and applicants can be overlooked. Having candidates apply by mail or in person are other options.

Set aside time to review each candidate's information to assess their fit for the job. Often, the first review will be to eliminate those who are obviously not qualified. For the next set of reviews, it is useful to have a checklist of key requirements to help you identify those who might be a good fit. You may have to sort through the applications several times to identify the top prospects. Eventually, you will have a short list of candidates to be interviewed.

Assess Likely Candidates

A résumé or job application tells you only so much about a person. To evaluate a candidate, you need to meet them and assess whether they are truly a good fit for your company.

The primary means of assessment is through an interview, usually conducted face to face. If applicants are not locally based, some recruiters conduct meetings by telephone or video conference to save inconveniencing the candidates and to avoid travel costs, which are often borne by the hiring company.

If certain qualifications are bona fide requirements of the job, some companies administer tests to measure candidates' knowledge, skills, physical abilities, and so on. Personality assessments are also popular with some hiring managers.

Interviews

Before you interview applicants, use the job description as a guide to determine what questions will be helpful in assessing their qualifications.

Do what you can to put candidates at ease. The interview is not a test but a two-way conversation to determine if there is a good fit on both sides. You expect applicants to arrive on time, so do not keep them waiting. Begin with a friendly greeting and small talk about neutral subjects like the weather or the traffic. Offer coffee, water, or another beverage. Make sure the interview room is tidy and free of distractions. A desk strewn with papers and a computer monitor open to a spreadsheet may give the wrong impression. A clean desk with a copy of the candidate's application says nothing is more important at this moment than your conversation.

To be fair, and to make your job easier, every candidate should be asked the same questions and in the same order. This will also help you to justify a hiring decision if an unsuccessful candidate claims that you have discriminated against them. Do not ask questions unrelated to the job requirements because they may be interpreted as discriminatory. Remember, it is illegal to discriminate, based on the prohibited grounds of discrimination in the *Human Rights Code*. Even an innocent enquiry can be interpreted as discriminatory. For example, a friendly question about a candidate's children may be interpreted as an attempt to determine availability for overtime work. It could lead to a charge of discrimination based on family status if the person is not hired. If the job requires significant overtime, ask each candidate about their ability to work overtime on short notice.

You may want to conduct a team interview. One person asks questions of the candidate while other team members concentrate on the answers.

Using one or more standard interview techniques might be helpful. You could, for example, use competency-based, behavioural, and/or situational interviews.

Competency-based interviews determine whether the candidates have the skills for the job. Applicants might be asked to answer technical questions, solve hypothetical problems, or undertake job-related tests.

Behavioural interviews elicit information about the candidates' previous experience and behaviours. Further probing questions will provide additional information. For example, if the job requires someone who is a good problem-solver, a question might be "tell me about the most difficult problem you have encountered at work." Additional questions might include "What made it so difficult for you? How did you approach the solution? Who did you depend on for advice? What did you learn from that experience? How might you have approached it differently?"

Situational interviews present candidates with hypothetical situations based on actual job requirements and ask them what they would do in such circumstances. The challenge with this type of interview is that candidates can usually guess the right answer so further probing is necessary. For example, you might ask, "Why would you do it this way? What challenges do you anticipate? What would you do if this solution did not work?"

Skills Tests

If specific skills are important, candidates can be asked to complete tests of their abilities. For example, they might be asked to complete a written test, participate in an interview in a required second language, or operate job-related equipment. Various companies offer pre-employment assessment software. Any test you ask a candidate to complete must be a valid means of assessing job-related competencies.

Personality Assessments

Personality assessments have become popular tools for matching people to positions. The premise is that certain behavioural traits are predictors of high performance in specific jobs. Assessment companies use questionnaires completed by control groups of successful workers in those jobs. Through a rigorous validation process, their responses are used to create profiles of common traits that can predict success. After candidates complete the questionnaires, their results are compared to the appropriate profiles. It is also possible to use the tool to develop company-specific models if there is a large enough employee population to develop profiles.

If used correctly, personality assessments can provide you with further insights into each candidate. The danger is in relying too heavily on the assessments. A candidate who does not fit the profile will not necessarily be unsuccessful in the job. A skilled interviewer can use the tool to probe for more information and obtain a better understanding of the candidate's strengths.

Try an on-line search for *personality assessments* to find information about tools such as Predictive Index (PI), the Hogan Personality Inventory (HPI), the DiSC® Profile, and The Birkman Method®, to name four.

While it is important to take time to find the right fit, if your hiring process takes too long, applicants may no longer be available. Keep candidates informed of your progress. You might say, "We are conducting initial interviews this week. If you are selected for a second interview, you should hear from us by...." If there is any delay in the process, inform candidates and advise them of the new deadline.

Select the Right Person

When you have completed your interviews, you should have one or more applicants who are a potential fit for the job.

Evaluate each candidate and conduct appropriate background checks. This will take time, so make sure you continue to keep them informed of the process.

Evaluate the Candidates

Review your notes for each person to compare their strengths. At this stage, you might bring them back for second interviews, perhaps with a different person. Some companies have the finalists meet the work group so that their potential peers can provide feedback to the hiring manager.

Conduct Background and Reference Checks

Nobody should be offered a position until their previous employment and qualifications have been verified and references have been checked. According to a company called Hire Right, 85 percent of employers have caught applicants falsifying their résumés.

If specific educational qualifications are important, ask candidates to submit copies of college or university transcripts. These should be sent to you directly from the relevant educational institutions.

Advise candidates that you will be contacting former employers and ask for the names of referees and for permission to contact them. Assure the applicants that the current employer will not be contacted unless a job is offered and accepted. A written offer of employment should include a provision that the offer is subject to receipt of a positive reference from this employer.

If a candidate has given you the name of a referee, you can expect the reference to be a positive one, but if you have specific questions to ask, you can often tell from the way they are answered if the referee is being honest or evasive.

A reference check can be done verbally, or in writing, using standard questions to elicit the information you need:

> ➤ Determine the referee's relationship to the employee (e.g., supervisor, co-worker, or human resources manager). This helps to evaluate the referee's answers.
> ➤ If possible, ask the referee to confirm dates of employment, job title(s), responsibilities, and the candidate's reason for leaving the company.
> ➤ Ask about the candidate's strengths and needs for improvement (the term *weaknesses* is frowned on in human resources circles).
> ➤ Ask the referee, if possible, to confirm attendance records and timeliness.

If you have specific concerns about a candidate's suitability, tailor questions accordingly. I have sometimes described the job and asked the referees if they thought the candidate would be a good fit, and why they believe this to be so.

When speaking to former managers, you could ask if they would rehire the employee and if not, why not.

A final question might be "Is there anything else you can tell me that a prospective employer would want to know?"

Employers may require a written authorization from the candidate before providing references, so you may wish to have a consent form available for the applicant's signature. Other employers may have a policy of not providing references, which makes it more difficult to perform your due diligence. You will have to decide whether the lack of this reference is enough to decline offering the position.

Another way to verify a candidate's credentials is to use a background screening company. Such companies offer various options including checking references, verifying employment history and educational qualifications, searching for criminal records (if warranted and permitted under the *Police Record Checks Reform Act, 2015*), and reviewing credit history. They can also obtain a driver's abstract if driving is an essential part of the job.

Make Your Decision

Select the person who best fits your needs. It is unlikely that anyone will be a perfect fit for the job. HR professionals often suggest that companies "hire for strengths, hire for potential, hire for attitude; you can teach skills."

Take your time and consider all relevant factors. Sometimes, we make the mistake of hiring people because we like their personality when we should be hiring to fit the job. It is not necessary to be best friends with employees; you just need to be able to work with them.

In the rare event that none of the candidates is a good fit, consider restarting the process. A bad hire is worse than no hire.

Make an Offer of Employment

When you have selected the candidate you want, offer the position verbally and follow up in writing. Make sure the written offer is the same as what has been conveyed verbally, and that it is accurate. This letter will form part of the employment contract, so if anything is missing or incorrect, change it before the candidate formally accepts the offer (in writing).

Give the person a few days to respond. Some applicants will be ready to accept right away, while others may want time to review the offer. Be prepared for the candidate to negotiate at this stage. While the most common request relates to salary, others might include more vacation time, a change in hours, even accommodation for a previously undisclosed disability.

Once the position has been filled, it is common courtesy to contact unsuccessful candidates. You are not obliged to tell them why they were not selected but you should thank them for their time and explain that another candidate was found to be a better fit for the job. Do not say that you will keep their résumé on file unless there is a real expectation that they might be suitable for another position in the near future. It is dishonest and hurts your reputation.

Your offer of employment will include a start date; in most cases it should be at least two weeks in the future to allow the candidate to give appropriate notice to their current employer. Staying connected with the person during this time makes the new hire feel part of the team. You might keep them up to date on the status of projects they will be working on, meet for coffee, or include them in an invitation to a job-related social event. Updates should be brief, and coffee and social events voluntary. You are not entitled to impose on their time. If you have other employees, ensure they know details like the name, position, and start date of their new co-worker, and encourage them to make the person feel welcome.

How to Compete with Larger Organizations

A small business may not be able to compete with larger organizations on pay and benefits but could have other advantages in attracting good candidates.

Some people prefer to work for a small business. Others may have specific requirements of a potential employer, which you can meet. During interviews, find out what is important to each person. If your organization meets those expectations, pay may not be their most important priority.

Consider hiring older candidates who have a wealth of technical knowledge and experience. Some will be looking for salaries to match their experience, but others may be more interested in challenging work. They may welcome the opportunity, for example, to set up a new department in a growing company.

Give some thought to how you appear to potential employees. Is your website appealing? Is your recruitment process professional and welcoming? Do you call when you say you will? Are you honest in what you can offer? What perks might be of interest to candidates?

CHAPTER 4

Preparing For The New Employee

The better prepared you are to welcome a new hire, the more comfortable they will be on the first day. If this is your first employee, you will need to make certain preparations before they start work. These might include setting up your payroll and record-keeping processes, registering with the Workplace Safety and Insurance Board (WSIB) if required, organizing the workspace, or making arrangements for the employee to work from home.

Some of these preparations are mandatory. For example, you will have 10 days to register with WSIB and up to 46 days to make your first payroll remittance to the CRA (depending on the employee's start date). On their first day, you should provide the employee with copies of employment standards and safety information.

Set up Payroll

Paying employees involves more than writing a cheque or making a direct deposit. As an employer, you will be responsible for registering a payroll account, deducting payroll taxes, and making monthly remittances to the CRA. You will also have to maintain financial records in accordance with generally accepted accounting principles (GAAP). The CRA applies financial penalties, including interest if appropriate, for employers whose remittances are late or inaccurate.

The details of your payroll responsibilities as an employer are available on the agency's website. Some essential requirements are as follows.

Establish a Payroll Account

Establish a payroll account with the CRA before the first remittance is due. This can be done through the agency's website or by telephone (the number is listed on their website). You can add this account to an existing CRA business number. If you do not have a business number, one will be assigned along with your payroll account.

Obtain the Employee's Social Insurance Number

Once you hire a person, you must ensure they are legally entitled to work in Canada. This is done by requesting a valid Social Insurance Number (SIN) from the new employee within three days after the day on which their employment begins, and keeping this number on file. A best practice is to obtain the SIN card or confirmation letter and make a photocopy for the confidential employee file.

A SIN beginning with a 9 indicates that the candidate has been issued a temporary permit to work in Canada, and there is an expiry date. You are required to confirm that the employee is authorized to work for you and has a valid immigration document. Further details are available on the Canada Revenue Agency website.

Deductions and Remittances

You are required to make certain deductions from employees' pay, and remit payment to the CRA. In some cases, you will also have to submit an employer contribution. Remittances are generally due by the 15th of the month following the one in which they were taken. These deductions include

➤ **Income tax.** Deducted at source. Employees are required to complete the CRA's Form TD1 Personal Tax Credits Return so the company can determine the amount of tax to be withheld from pay.

➤ **Taxable benefits.** You must calculate and withhold tax on certain employer-provided benefits such as life insurance.

➤ **CPP and EI.** Both the employer and the employee contribute to CPP and EI. The employee's contributions are withheld from pay and remitted along with the employer's contributions.

You need the employee's written authorization or a court order to make any other deductions. For example, an employee's written authorization would be required to deduct the employee portion of premiums for company benefits. A court order might be issued for the garnishment of wages.

However, even with a signed authorization, an employer is not permitted to deduct from wages an amount to cover a loss due to faulty work or, in some cases, lost or stolen property.

Employer Health Tax (Ontario)

In Ontario, employers pay a provincial employer health tax if their total payroll exceeds the amount eligible for exemption. Details are available on Ontario's Ministry of Finance website.

Records for Employees

An employer must provide employees with the following records.

Statement of Earnings. Give each employee a statement of earnings for each pay period, showing the gross amount earned, all deductions, and the net income for both the current period and the year to date.

T4. For each calendar year, issue each employee a T4 slip reporting their annual earnings and withholdings and file a T4 information return to the CRA on or before the last day of February of the following year.

Records Retention

Retain paper and electronic payroll records as specified by the CRA and other government agencies (currently, for a minimum of six years).

Establish How You Will Process Payroll

You can process your own payroll or outsource it. If you choose to do payroll in-house, use a spreadsheet, accounting software, or commercially available payroll software for convenience.

In setting up a spreadsheet enter all relevant information for each employee. This includes identifying information such as name, address, SIN, as well as the information required to calculate each employee's gross pay, deductions, and net pay. You will have to record other data such as hours worked for hourly workers, vacation time earned and taken, vacation dollars paid, statutory holiday time taken and paid, and overtime hours worked and paid. Where possible, include formulas to make calculations. You can also set up any forms you will need, such as a statement of earnings, and export data from the spreadsheet to populate the forms. The main challenge in doing your own payroll is keeping up to date with legislation.

If you are using an accounting software package, it likely has a payroll module in which all the setup work has been done for you. If you are working with an accountant, you can add payroll processing to their responsibilities.

Commercially available software solutions are programmed to make all necessary payroll calculations and to automatically create documents such as pay statements and T4s. Some have the capability to make direct deposits to employees' bank accounts. Some companies offer their payroll software free to small businesses.

You can also outsource the work to a full-service payroll processing company. Most have payroll solutions for small businesses with as few as one employee.

Due diligence is necessary to ensure that any company you deal with keeps data secure and respects Canadian privacy legislation.

Establish a Record-Keeping Process

The *Employment Standards Act, 2000* specifies the information you must keep for each employee. This includes identifying information like the person's name, address, hire date, and SIN. You are also required to keep records on virtually every aspect of each worker's employment (e.g., pay, vacations, leaves of absence, termination date, and training records). This information must be securely stored either in confidential files or in encrypted electronic systems.

Human Resource Information Systems

A human resource information system (HRIS) is software used to store and manipulate employee data electronically. It allows you to quickly retrieve stored information about any employee and automatically populate forms, generate reports, or export data to a spreadsheet.

While a small employer does not need a complex software program to manage employee information, data is easier to source and process when stored electronically. Another advantage of storing information electronically from the beginning is that when your company is large enough to need a more complex HRIS, the historical records you need to input can be uploaded.

As your business grows, you might want to purchase a commercially available HRIS that automates virtually every aspect of employment management. Such systems are updated regularly for compliance with legislation and often come with help-line support. Many companies offer affordable options for small businesses. As well, payroll service companies like ADP and Ceridian include integrated HRIS programs, so that any changes made that affect an employee's pay can be automatically downloaded to the payroll module.

Larger organizations often use enterprise resource planning (ERP) systems with built-in HR modules. These allow data to be shared by different departments and used as needed. In one simple example, a warehouse worker would log in to the supply chain module on arrival and log out before leaving the premises. Their hours of work would be calculated electronically and accessed by the HR and payroll modules.

This type of direct access puts information into the hands of all who need it and reduces the risk of transposition errors.

When selecting a commercial system, it is important to learn where the information will reside, and what safeguards are in place to protect personal records. Data stored outside Canada could be subject to the laws of, and accessed by, foreign governments.

As noted in Chapter 1, employee information must be protected. The Information and Privacy Commissioner of Ontario has indicated that electronic records containing personal information should be stored and encrypted on a password-protected disk or CD rather than on the hard drive of a laptop or of a home computer. Only those with the proper authority within the business should have access to employee information. Include normal IT backup and offsite storage procedures to avoid losing electronic records.

Register With the Workplace Safety and Insurance Board

In Ontario, the WSIB, formerly the Workers' Compensation Board (WCB), provides accident and illness coverage for the employees of member companies.

Most provincially regulated employers in Ontario must register with the WSIB within 10 days of hiring their first employee, and pay a monthly premium based on the organization's size and industry. Organizations not required to register have the option to do so. A list of exempt organizations is available on the WSIB website.

If an employee suffers a work-related injury or an illness, thereby requiring medical attention or losing income, the employer must report the incident to the WSIB within three calendar days of learning of the event.

The WSIB provides employees who are injured at work with compensation for loss of earnings, payment of health care costs, payment toward a non-economic loss, or survivor benefits. In most cases, an employee covered by WSIB does not have the right to sue their employer for a work-related accident.

If your employees perform work on clients' premises, the clients may request a WSIB clearance from you. This information certifies that the workers are covered by WSIB, and premiums are up to date. Clearances may be ordered electronically through WSIB's eClearance service (available on their website) and are valid for 90 days.

> If employees work in more than one province, they must be covered by workers' compensation in each province where they work.

Information for Employees

Employers must provide the following information for employees. Further details, including how to obtain copies of the posters, are available on the website of the Ministry of Labour, Training and Skills Development. If your employees are based at home, send them copies of these documents, and post copies on an electronic data-sharing site such as an intranet or Dropbox.

The *Employment Standards Act, 2000* requires employers to give the most recent version of the poster Employment Standards in Ontario: Fair at Work Ontario to each person within 30 days of their becoming an employee.

To comply with the *Occupational Health and Safety Act*, employers must post Health & Safety at Work: Prevention Starts Here in the workplace. This poster outlines the rights and responsibilities of workers, supervisors, and employers on the job. It also includes a Ministry of Labour telephone number for reporting critical injuries, fatalities, and work refusals and for obtaining information about workplace health and safety.

Companies whose workers are covered by the WSIB must display the In Case of Injury poster (Form 82). The Board sends the poster and an employer guide to registered employers.

The *Occupational Health and Safety Act* also requires that the following be displayed in the workplace:

> ➢ A copy of the *Occupational Health and Safety Act*
> ➢ The names and work locations of the Joint Health and Safety Committee. A Joint Health and Safety Committee is only required if a company has 20 employees or more or if a designated substance regulation applies to the workplace.
> ➢ For employers with more than five employees, copies of health and safety, workplace violence, and workplace harassment policies developed and maintained by the company.

Prepare for Employees Working from Home

If your new employee will be working from home, the employment laws still apply to them. You need to determine how you will, for example, monitor their compliance with employment standards or your policies and procedures, ensure they have a safe workplace, and protect the confidentiality of information.

Determine who will be responsible for supplies and equipment and whether the employee will use their own office furniture, computer, and supplies. Establish whether they will be reimbursed for consumables like paper and printer ink. Confirm that your business insurance covers an employee working from home.

CHAPTER 5

Welcoming The New Employee

The first few weeks on a new job are crucial to making the employee feel comfortable in the new role. Managers evaluate the employee's suitability for the business, and the employee assesses the organization's fit with their expectations. Various sources have reported that up to 20 percent of staff turnover occurs within the first 45 days of employment. The more you do to support the new recruit during this period, the more likely that you will have a happy, committed hire. The practices of employee orientation and onboarding are designed for this purpose.

Orientation

Orientation should take place in the first few days after hire. It is intended to make an employee feel welcome, to confirm the new employee's role, and to explain company policies.

On the first day, introduce the new employee to team members and other staff, if there are any. Provide a brief overview of the business and its policies and procedures.

Larger organizations will include a tour of the facilities during orientation.

Review the employee's job description and responsibilities and answer any questions.

Have the employee sign any necessary documents, such as a confidentiality agreement and benefits application forms. The purpose of each document should be explained, and the employee should be given copies of everything they have signed.

Ensure that the employee's workstation, tools, phone, and other supplies are available and in good working order.

It can be helpful to assign somebody who can answer questions for the new team member and who will make sure that they are included in group activities such as lunch and breaks.

Onboarding

Onboarding is intended to help the employee integrate into the organization and become an effective member of the team.

Check in with the new employee on a regular basis to answer any questions and ask how they are progressing. Larger organizations often assign the new hire a mentor who can offer guidance and resolve problems for the first few weeks.

Introduce the employee to clients and suppliers as appropriate. Establish a training schedule and make sure training is accomplished according to the schedule.

The better organized and prepared you are, the easier it will be for the new employee to become comfortable in the position and in your organization.

CHAPTER 6

Compensation

Compensation is the material value one receives in return for services provided to an employer. For many people, it is the primary reason they seek employment. To encourage employee retention, the compensation you offer should be appropriate for the responsibilities and demands of the position. At the same time, it must fit your budget.

Compensation includes base pay (regular pay/salary), variable pay (commission/bonus), and other elements such as shift differentials, overtime pay, on-call pay, and stock options.

Determining how to compensate employees is an art, not a science. Early in my career, I found it frustrating to have collected vast amounts of survey data, and still not know the correct market rates for positions in my company. So many variables affected decisions. In some cases, the jobs being analysed were not an exact match to survey benchmarks. In addition, results differed from one survey to another, plus I could not find survey matches for all positions. There is no right answer. You set compensation rates based on your analysis of the market and your best judgment.

Understanding the Market

You can outsource market research. Professional companies providing compensation analysis services can be found through an on-line search. Alternatively, a small start-up business wishing to conduct its own research can obtain information at little or no cost. A trusted employment agency should have a good feel for the local market, and some of the larger agencies publish salary guides. On-line sites like PayScale (payscale.com) and Glassdoor (glassdoor.ca) also publish salary and wage information. The Government of Canada job bank has a searchable database of wages and salaries. When using these on-line sites, you should ensure that you match position descriptions, not job titles. You also want to be clear about the elements included in each report. The Government of Canada, for example, includes both salaries and commissions in its reported wage data. Use multiple sources to get a good feel for the market.

Another way to establish pay rates for specific jobs is through a quick telephone survey of local businesses. Some may be willing to share information.

A comparison of the data collected should suggest a competitive market rate, and you can decide whether to use that rate or one slightly higher or lower. Factors to consider are your budget, candidates' expectations, and how closely the jobs researched match your own circumstances. You might, for example, offer a higher rate if you do not offer employee benefits or a lower rate for a job that requires less knowledge or skill than those used as benchmarks. Some employers decide to pay at a higher rate to attract top performers.

Salary Ranges

When there are multiple incumbents in the same position, it is common to establish a salary range with a minimum, midpoint, and maximum to allow for various levels of experience or performance. New, inexperienced employees can be paid at the lower end of the range, and top performers at the higher end. In a typical salary range, the market rate becomes the midpoint, with the minimum and maximum being 80 percent and 120 percent of the midpoint, respectively. These criteria may need to be adjusted. I once set a salary range on this basis and could not attract entry-level candidates at the minimum of the range.

Companies that start new employees at the range's minimum sometimes establish milestones for increasing their pay as they become more proficient over a period such as the first six, twelve, and eighteen months.

Market rates for commission and bonus plans (variable pay) can be determined the same way.

Develop a Compensation Philosophy

As a business grows, you may find it helpful to develop a compensation philosophy that outlines the purpose of the pay program (e.g., to hire and retain top performers), establishes a means of ensuring fairness and equity in compensation, and defines how pay decisions are to be made. Details and examples of compensation philosophies can be found on-line.

When an organization hires its tenth employee, compensation becomes more challenging, due to the need to comply with pay equity legislation in Ontario. Jobs will have to be identified as male-dominated, female-dominated, or neutral, and compared based on skill, effort, responsibility, and working conditions.

Variable Pay

Commission and bonus plans for variable pay are incentives to achieve specific goals. Commission plans are designed for salespeople, and bonus plans for those in other fields.

I have heard salespeople referred to as either *hunters* or *gatherers*. Hunters are those whose primary role is to sell products to new and existing clients. They are always on the hunt for new business, hence the name. Hunters may welcome, and do well on, straight commission plans. Their only form of compensation is commission, and the more they sell, the more they earn. They may also focus their efforts on products with a higher commission return, so be careful how you structure your incentive plans.

Gatherers are salespeople who are expected to develop long-term relationships with customers, usually where a sale is more complex, requires significant involvement by the salespeople, and takes a long time to complete. Because gatherers are not able to make quick sales, their compensation tends to be based on salary plus commission. While commissioned salespeople are not eligible for overtime pay, those on salary plus commission may be.

Bonuses are designed to encourage and reward employees for achieving specific goals. These goals should be measurable, and within the employees' control. They can be structured for individuals or for teams. Where it is not possible to measure an individual's or a team's contribution, an employer may give a company-wide year-end bonus if the business meets its objectives. A bonus calculated as a percentage of salary recognizes that those in higher positions make a greater contribution to the organization's success. Giving everyone the same bonus amount recognizes that success is a team effort.

Be careful of unintended consequences. For example, if a support team receives bonuses for controlling expenses, they may have a conflict with sales teams. One group is keeping a tight rein on expenses while the other is focused on selling at any cost. The success of one group may negatively impact the achievement of the other's variable pay plan, causing conflict. Commission and bonus plans for various parts of the company should be complementary.

The design of plans will depend on the goals for your business. A quick internet search for *designing a commission structure* or *designing a bonus plan* can get you started.

Executive Compensation

Executive compensation plans are not common in smaller companies. They are designed to provide rewards to senior managers for actual results. As well as salary and bonus, the plans include long-term incentives such as stock options.

Other perquisites designed to attract and retain top executives can include enhanced benefit and pension plans, and company-owned vehicles.

CHAPTER 7

Benefits

Legislated Benefits

Certain employee benefits are prescribed by federal and provincial legislation.

Canada Pension Plan

Participation in the CPP is mandatory for all employees, except those in the Province of Quebec, who are covered by the Quebec Pension Plan. Both the employee and the employer pay premiums based on the employee's earnings. Premiums are remitted to the CRA monthly. The Canada Pension Plan Investment Board is responsible for managing the plan's funds.

Employment Insurance

All employees must participate in the EI program. Both the employee and the employer pay premiums based on the employee's earnings. Premiums are remitted to the CRA monthly. When an employee leaves the company, the employer must issue a record of employment (ROE) and send a copy to Service Canada. Details are available on the Service Canada website. The ROE is used to determine eligibility for EI benefits, as well as to detect fraudulent claims.

Government Mandated Leaves

The provincial government mandates that leaves of absence be made available to employees in Ontario Eligibility may depend on length of service. In most cases, although leaves are without pay, employees continue to earn credit for seniority and length of service and are eligible to continue in company-sponsored benefit plans. Please refer to the employment standards website of the Ministry of Labour, Training and Skills Development for details and updates.

In some cases, employees may be able to apply for loss-of-earnings benefits through the EI program or the CPP.

Ontario Health Insurance Plan (OHIP)

The Ontario Health Insurance Plan (OHIP) is a government-sponsored benefit. Although the healthcare OHIP provides is free at point of service, OHIP itself is partially financed through the employer health tax and a health premium paid annually by Ontario residents whose taxable income exceeds a specified amount.

Employer-Sponsored Benefits

Employer-sponsored benefits, also known as supplementary benefits (i.e., supplementary to government benefits like OHIP) are a form of compensation offered to employees over and above regular salary or wages. Such benefits may help to attract and retain employees but can be costly. Even larger organizations are rethinking traditional programs that include group life, health, and dental insurance, as well as a defined benefit pension plan.

Before introducing employer-sponsored benefits, you may wish to consult a qualified benefits consultant for suggestions that fit your needs and ability to pay. Questions they can answer include:

➤ Why do I want to offer a benefits plan?
➤ What type of plan can I afford?
➤ What benefits are most likely to help me attract and retain employees?
➤ What do people want versus what do they need?
➤ How should I design the plan? Which benefits should be mandatory, which should be optional, and who pays the premiums (employer, employee, or both)?

Traditional employer benefits plans continue to be popular with employees, but so are more flexible offerings such as health care spending accounts. Employee assistance plans have also become popular.

Group Life Insurance

Group life insurance is a common benefit and is affordable because it provides coverage at group rates. As it is a pooled benefit (i.e., in a pool with other companies), large claims do not cause significant increases in one company's premium rates. Plan options might include basic life insurance for the employee, dependents' life insurance, and supplementary life insurance. If the company pays the premium for group life insurance, the cost is a taxable benefit to employees and must be recorded on the employees' pay statements and their statements of earnings for tax purposes (T4s).

Basic life insurance covers only the employee and is calculated as a multiple of the employee's base pay or total direct compensation (salary plus bonus/commission). The premiums may be paid by the company, by the employee, or by both in a shared arrangement.

Dependents' life insurance for the spouse and children of the employee is typically a set amount, such as $10,000 for the spouse and $5,000 for each child. This may be an optional benefit, with premiums paid by the company, by the employee, or shared.

In addition, a company may offer an optional supplementary life insurance plan for the employee and/or spouse. Premiums are at group rates and depend on variables such as the insured's age and gender. Premiums for supplementary life insurance are usually paid by the employee.

Group Health and Dental Insurance

Group health and dental insurance covers many of the expenses not included in the provincial health plan. The business pays a premium to an insurance company to cover the cost of benefits paid out plus an administrative fee. While popular with employees, it is becoming increasingly expensive. Health and dental insurance premiums are experience-rated, meaning that the cost of claims paid by the insurance company in the current year will be used to determine premiums for the following year. The more claims there are, the higher the monthly costs will be the next year. Many employers require employees to pay a portion of the premiums (for example, 60 percent employer/40 percent employee). Some plans are structured so that the employee pays all costs up to a certain amount (a deductible) before the insurance coverage comes into effect.

Examples of group health insurance coverage include

> ➤ approved prescription drugs (plans may specify generic only).
> ➤ ambulance services.
> ➤ private or semi-private hospital coverage (OHIP pays for a ward).
> ➤ out-of-province/country emergency medical services.
> ➤ paramedical services like physiotherapy, massage, and psychotherapy.
> ➤ vision care.

Examples of group dental insurance coverage include

> ➤ basic dental (checkups, cleanings, and fillings), which covers 80 to 100 percent of costs.
> ➤ major restorative services (crowns), which might cover 50 percent of costs.
> ➤ orthodontics: often only for children and with a lifetime maximum amount.

Administrative Services Only Contracts

An alternative to a traditional insured benefits plan is an administrative services only (ASO) contract. While the employer pays a nominal amount for administration and adjudication of claims, there is no annual premium. If a claim is approved, the employer pays the cost. This is cheaper in the short term but exposes the business to the expense of potentially large payouts for claims.

Sick Benefits

When employees are unable to work due to illness or a disability, they do not have to be paid. However, some companies offer sick benefits, which are designed to provide an income during either a short-term or long-term absence from work.

If a person is disabled, they may apply for EI and could be eligible to receive up to 15 weeks of EI sickness benefits. If the disability is severe and prolonged and prevents the employee from being able to work at any job on a regular basis, the employee may apply for disability benefits available through the CPP.

An employee may be unable to work, but not yet eligible for benefits through EI or the CPP. While human rights legislation prevents you from terminating the worker's employment due to a disability, you have no legal obligation to pay them. However, to leave someone with no means of support or income for a time is a difficult decision and can reflect poorly on the company. You may want your benefits plan to include paid sick days and/or disability insurance.

Paid Sick days (also known as sick time) are paid days off on account of sickness or illness. This allows the worker time to rest and recuperate, and it encourages people to stay home when they are sick, so they do not infect others. While some employers require doctors' notes as a condition of payment, the Canadian Medical Association discourages this practice. It places a burden on doctors and discourages people from taking time off when they are ill and potentially infectious.

From a human resources perspective, requiring doctors' notes suggests a lack of trust in employees. You will create a better work environment by trusting employees and dealing with offenders individually.

Short-term disability (STD) insurance pays a portion of the employee's salary for a defined length of time (e.g., up to 13 or 26 weeks). Coverage may be administered through an insurance company (insured plans) or directly by the company (self-administered plans). Some STD plans begin payout after a qualifying period (e.g. 14, 30,

60, or 90 days). Insured plans without a waiting period tend to have higher premiums because they will have more claims. Self-administered plans with no waiting period should make it clear to employees what types of illness or disability qualify for the benefit. One advantage of an insured plan is that the decision to approve or deny benefits is out of the employer's hands.

Long-term disability (LTD) insurance pays a portion of the employee's salary if they are disabled for an extended period or permanently. A typical plan would come into effect after the expiration of a waiting period, which may be covered by the company's short-term disability plan. LTD premiums are commonly paid by the employees, and any benefit received is tax-free. If the employer pays the premium, the benefit is taxable and the premium must be reported on the employee's pay slip and T4. Coverage for LTD is typically provided through a third-party insurer. Plan sponsors (i.e., employers) should consider structuring coverage such that the CPP is the first payor, so CPP disability benefits will be taken into consideration when calculations are made regarding a claimant's eligibility for LTD. Many employees will be eligible for both.

Insurers will typically extend LTD coverage for a terminated employee during the notice period required by employment standards legislation (up to 8 weeks), but not for any additional notice period required under common law. A terminated employee who becomes disabled after the first 8 weeks of the notice period, and has no LTD coverage, may be successful in suing the employer for damages. Speak to your insurance provider about ways to extend LTD coverage during the full common law notice period.

Employee Assistance Plans

Some employers are offering coverage for mental/ emotional health care through employee assistance plans (EAPs). The goal is to help employees cope with stress from personal issues that affect their work and well-being, to reduce absenteeism and turnover, and to foster a more productive workplace.

EAPs provide confidential counselling to employees and their families for a range of issues such as financial problems, legal needs, health issues, separation, and divorce. The claimant is offered free and confidential support, information, and advice. The employer pays a set fee, usually based on the number of employees, and receives statistical reports on the number and type of services accessed. These reports can be useful in recognizing trends.

Other Benefits

Employers looking for creative ways to attract and retain employees may offer other types of benefits such as personal days or flexible benefits.

Personal days are paid days off work to be used when an employee is not ill but has another legitimate reason to need time off. Examples might include a moving day, visiting a relative who is gravely ill, or attending a child's graduation.

Flexible benefit plans allow employees to select from a pool of employer-sponsored benefits to suit their individual needs. A Health Care Spending Account (HCSA) may be the most affordable for a small employer. In a HCSA, a pre-determined amount is allocated to each employee at the beginning of the calendar year or an alternative benefit year. The employee can use the funds to pay for any health and dental expenses that are approved for a HCSA under CRA guidelines. The plan may allow for unused monies to be carried forward to following years. A HCSA gives employees the flexibility to allocate funds toward expenses that are important to them.

The perceived value of benefits depends on employees' needs. Things valued by employees might include paid tuition, paid education leave, extra time off, flexible hours, telecommuting (working from home), health care memberships, or subsidized day care.

A Note on Taxable Benefits

The CRA deems certain employer-provided items to be taxable benefits. Examples include life insurance premiums, meals, parking, car allowances, personal use of business vehicles, and gifts over a certain amount. The value of each must be calculated and included on the employees' T4s. The CRA website has an employers' guide to taxable benefits and allowances.

Retirement Benefits

While employers are not required to provide company pensions or other retirement savings plans, offering employees peace of mind about the future can contribute to an environment where workers are content and productive.

If employers do provide retirement benefits, most plans must be registered with the CRA. Legislation and issues around retirement savings plans are complex, and beyond the scope of this book, but the following material provides basic information. Employers are encouraged to research options carefully and speak to a qualified advisor before implementing a retirement plan.

Registered Pension Plans

There are two types of registered pension plans: defined benefit and defined contribution.

In a **defined benefit pension plan**, the employer commits to providing a pension amount based on a formula (typically the employee's age and length of service at retirement). Under this plan, the employer bears the risk if there is insufficient money in the plan to pay all retirees. On the other hand, when there is a pension surplus (greater funds in the plan than required to fund the pensions of all current and future retirees), the employer may be able to take a contribution holiday, if it is permitted in the plan.

In a **defined contribution pension plan**, the employee and/or the employer make regular contributions to the employee's pension plan, and the employee decides how to invest the money within the options available. At retirement, the employee uses the funds accumulated to purchase a retirement product (an annuity or a life income fund). The employee bears the risk if there are insufficient funds for retirement, but the employer has a responsibility to ensure that suitable fund options and investment education are provided to all plan members.

As of 2012, employees are fully vested immediately upon joining a defined pension plan (i.e., they have full entitlement to the pension amount available through their own and the employer's contributions).

Other Options for Retirement Plans

Other retirement savings options include employer-sponsored Pooled Registered Pension Plans (PRPPs), Deferred Profit-Sharing Plans (DPSPs), Group Registered Retirement Savings Plans (GRRSPs), and Tax-Free Savings Accounts (TFSAs).

A **PRPP** holds assets pooled together from multiple participating employers and is administered by eligible Canadian corporations, such as insurance companies and banks. A PRPP may permit a member to make investment choices from among the options offered by the administrator.

In a **DPSP**, the company contributes to a plan on the employees' behalf from company profits. Contributions are tax-sheltered until withdrawn.

Employers may set up **GRRSPs** on behalf of employees. As with personal RRSPs, tax is deferred on contributions made through payroll deduction.

A business may also set up a group **TFSA**. Employees can make post-tax contributions to their accounts through payroll deduction. Any contributions made to an employee's account by the employer are considered taxable income for the employee and are tax deductible for the employer.

Retiree Insured Benefits Plans

Some employers allow employees to stay on their insured benefits plans (life, health, and dental insurance) after retirement, with the same or reduced coverage. This is valuable for older workers but can be costly for plan sponsors because people tend to require more medical services as they grow older. I know of one company that had more retirees than active employees enrolled in its benefits plans. A qualified consultant can help you structure a plan that works for a small employer.

CHAPTER 8

Human Resources Management

Having employees means you will need to spend a certain amount of your time dealing with issues such as training, coaching, and problem solving.

The importance of being a good manager is sometimes overlooked. If work is being done and turnover is not a problem, the business can seem to run smoothly for years. On the other hand, without good management problems may develop. For example, conflict can arise, employee motivation can drop, people may cover up their mistakes, absenteeism can increase, or people may quietly look for other work.

Ask five different employees what makes a good manager, and you are likely to get five different opinions. This is because everyone's needs and expectations are different and can change. An inexperienced employee may appreciate hands-on coaching. That same person, having gained experience and confidence, is likely to want more autonomy.

Personalities are also important. For some people, enforcement of rules is mandatory, while others may prefer to see rules as guidelines. There may be conflict when these two personalities interact, especially if one is the other's manager. If you develop a rapport with the people you work with, you will know how they prefer to be managed.

As a small employer, you have the benefit of being able to communicate with everyone on a personal level. Use that advantage to understand your workforce. Take an interest in their career aspirations and what motivates them. Recognize that employees are competent, intelligent adults with whom you have a contractual agreement.

If you do not have experience managing people, you will need to add management proficiency to your technical, professional, and entrepreneurial skills. Whether you are new to management or have experience, it may be helpful to take some relevant personal development courses. Make sure to do your due diligence when choosing a program. I have had positive experiences with the Canadian Management Centre and with continuing education programs at local community colleges and universities, as well as with recognized training companies.

An important aspect of managing people is providing feedback. Employees need to know when they are meeting or exceeding your expectation, and when they are not. Regular, ongoing, informal feedback is good because it reinforces or corrects behaviour as it occurs. ("Nice job on that report," "Thank you for stepping in and helping that customer," "There may have been a better way to handle that situation.")

More formal, written feedback is also important, and is accomplished through a performance review or, in serious situations, through a performance improvement plan.

Performance Reviews

Performance reviews done well help to improve communication with employees, provide them with feedback about their job performance, and identify training or developmental needs. Written reviews provide historical records of performance. They also provide important documentation to be used when making decisions about salary increases, promotions, and downsizing.

In recent years there has been a gradual shift from doing the traditional top-down annual review to a more effective, ongoing, two-way discussion. Managers might meet with each employee once a month, with a focus on employee development rather than evaluation. Employees who are not meeting expectations can be given timely feedback and guidance, and those who are doing well can be encouraged. Annual reviews may still be used. Documented monthly meetings will give managers valuable information on which to base their assessments.

I believe in allowing employees to provide a written response to a performance review, especially if they disagree with what the manager has written about them. As well as giving the employee an outlet for their opinion, the feedback provides the manager with valuable information for understanding the employee's motivation and expectations. It also provides an opportunity to improve communication.

Advice on performance management is readily available on-line, and training is available through colleges, universities, and professional consultants.

Performance Issues

When an employee is not meeting expectations, the first reaction is often to let the person go. Before getting to that point, a manager might try to help them to improve or to find a better job match within the organization.

The manager might start with a face-to-face conversation and, rather than opening with the performance issue, ask the employee what is going well and what problems are being encountered. In most cases, an employee will know that there are issues which need to be resolved. In this situation it should be easy for the manager to ask how the business can help, what training might be needed, and what roadblocks are impeding performance. Otherwise, after the initial conversation, the manager can raise the performance issue, and follow with the same questions: "How can I help? What training do you need? What roadblocks are impeding your work?" The manager and employee can then put a plan in place to provide the necessary training and support and to allow the manager to check in regularly to monitor the employee's progress.

An employee may be unable or unwilling to improve performance. If the person is unsuited for the job, it is best for all concerned to find a position that is a better fit, either within the organization or elsewhere. If there is an internal position available, both the employee and the organization benefit. The employee is more likely to be successful in a job more suited to their skills and the employer can find a better candidate to fill the vacated position. If the company has no suitable internal position, it is best to let the employee go so they can find more appropriate employment elsewhere.

When an employee does not acknowledge the need to improve, the manager may initiate a formal performance improvement plan (PIP). This involves providing the employee with written notice of what needs to improve, by when, what help will be provided, and what the consequences will be if expectations are not met. The manager should ensure that the promised help is provided and check in with the employee on a regular basis to monitor progress. If the plan is to terminate the person's employment if they do not succeed, it needs to be clearly stated. A well-managed PIP will help the employee make the required improvement or may provide the employer with the necessary documentation to terminate employment without expensive severance costs. The employee should be asked to sign the PIP to acknowledge that they have read and understood it.

When dealing with performance improvement issues, it is important to document everything. This documentation may be needed to establish cause for termination and be used in defence of an unjust dismissal claim by the employee. It is also a very good idea to involve an employment lawyer early in the process of establishing a PIP or initiating a termination to determine if you have sufficient cause to terminate the employment without providing the required employment standards or common law notice.

Salary Reviews

An effective performance management system will help to ensure fairness and to justify pay decisions. When you sit down with employees to discuss pay, they should already know how their performance has been evaluated and should have had an opportunity to discuss the rating with you. This way, there will be no surprises.

Many employees expect to have a salary increase at least annually. If they fall behind the market, they may start to look for work elsewhere. I would inform candidates during the interview process, or at the time you make an offer of employment, if increases are not an option in your business. Losing a potentially good prospect at this stage may be preferable to dealing with a disgruntled employee later.

If you do plan to offer pay increases, you will need to establish a budget, and decide how to allocate it. Various consulting firms publish actual percentage salary increases for the current year and projections for the following year, based on their survey data. Use the market research process outlined in Chapter 6 to determine what, if any, increase is appropriate.

You will want to factor in the impact of pay increases on expenses like payroll taxes, benefits costs, and overtime pay. In addition, this year's increases will inflate the budget for next year and create expectations for the future.

The simplest way to allocate the money is to give everyone the same percentage as a cost of living adjustment (COLA). A COLA is not tied to performance. It is based on a published measurement such as the Consumer Price Index (CPI).

On the other hand, the budget may be used to adjust low wages, to fund promotions, or to reward high performers. These pay raises are called a market adjustment, a promotional increase, and a merit increase, respectively. The first two are simple and straightforward to implement, but the third is more challenging.

When raises are based on merit, managers must be trained to make decisions based on employees' value to the organization. An effective performance review process will provide the information necessary to make such decisions.

To develop a plan for merit increases you can ask a series of questions. Will these increases be paid on a common review date, or on the anniversary of each person's hire? If on a common review date, will increases be prorated for new employees who have not been with you for a full year? How do you decide how to allocate the raises? As an example, assume there are five employees, all making $20 per hour. One is an acceptable employee, three are good, solid workers, and one stands out above the rest. If the merit budget is $2.50 per hour, you might decide to increase the hourly pay of the acceptable employee by 25 cents, each solid performer by 50 cents, and the star by 75 cents.

A clear, well-understood compensation policy will help employees to understand how their pay is determined and what kinds of increases are available. Some companies publish their market rates or pay ranges. Others prefer to keep this information confidential.

Promotions

When you decide that you need a supervisor or manager, your first impulse may be to promote the best worker in the group. Unfortunately, the skills and aptitudes that make a good worker are not always those that make an effective leader. Take time to develop a job description for the new position and assess candidates accordingly. As well as being able to understand the technical aspects of the job, supervisors need to be effective communicators and be able to objectively resolve disputes. They also need leadership, interpersonal and time management skills, to be good problem solvers, and to understand and support policies and procedures. Supervisors and managers also need to be accountable for their actions. Someone who enforces rules reluctantly and then blames decisions on senior management is not an asset to an organization.

A good employee development plan or succession plan will help to ensure that promotable employees are ready when an opportunity arises.

Employee Development Plans

An employee development plan is a process designed to help a person enhance their proficiency or gain new skills.

Planning can begin with a conversation about the individual's challenges, interests, and aspirations, or the manager's plans for the company. Together, the manager and employee establish goals, tools, and timelines. Tools for development might include external courses, mentoring and coaching, temporary reassignment, or any means by which a person can learn and enhance skills. Information about employee development plans is readily available on-line.

Succession Planning

Large companies create succession plans to ensure a smooth transition when a senior manager leaves. Small business owners may want to do the same for key employees or for when they, the employer, are planning to retire and want the business to continue under existing ownership. It involves identifying and mentoring subordinates, so they are ready to take on a particular position when someone leaves or is unavailable for an extended period.

In developing a succession plan, begin by asking yourself questions such as: Who is your second in command? Can that person step in at a moment's notice if needed? If not, what training or mentoring do you need to provide? Then establish an employee development plan as well as procedures to be followed when the need for succession arises. Use the same process to identify who would be available to move into the vacated position, and the training or mentoring they will require.

If you want help in creating such plans, a quick internet search for succession planning consultants will identify companies that offer this service.

Terminations

Terminating someone's employment can be among the most difficult responsibilities of a manager. The process is never easy but will go more smoothly if the manager is prepared.

As noted in Chapter 1, under common law, you can terminate a worker's employment at any time and for any reason as long as that reason does not contravene human rights legislation. For example, you can let somebody go because their work is not up to standard, but not if the person has a disability that can be accommodated to bring their performance to an acceptable level.

Termination may be without cause, meaning for reasons outside the employee's control, such as changes in job requirements or company downsizing, or it may be because the worker has done something that warrants immediate dismissal for cause.

Without Cause

Where there is no just cause to terminate the employment, you are legally required to provide notice, or pay in lieu of notice (termination pay), in accordance with employment standards legislation. Additional termination pay may also be warranted under common law if the employer has not contracted with the employee to limit their entitlement to only the minimums under the employment standards legislation.

Termination pay may be offered as a lump sum or as salary continuance. The terminated individual must also continue to receive employee benefits during the notice period.

Under the provincial *Employment Standards Act, 2000* companies with a payroll of at least $2.5 million must also provide severance pay if they have employed the individual for at least five years.

It is important to know the employee's entitlements under employment standards legislation as well as the organization's potential liability at common law. Using this information, prepare (or have legal counsel prepare) a letter to the employee which clearly states that the employment is being terminated and that explains any notice period, or the terms of payment in lieu of notice. It is not necessary to give a reason for the termination, other than to advise if it is without cause or for cause.

An employer may limit notice requirements to the minimums required by the employment standards legislation; doing this requires the use of a well-written contract of employment that is understood and agreed to by all employees. If no such contract exists, or if the courts determine that the contract is unenforceable, the amount of notice required will be guided by common law and can be significant. It is always advisable to have a lawyer review your employment contracts, and generally a good idea to consult a lawyer before terminating somebody's employment.

If notice of termination is given, the expectation is that the employee will continue to do their work during the notice period and will act with integrity. During this time, the employer might help the employee find alternate employment by allowing time off to attend interviews, networking with business colleagues to see if they have a suitable position for the individual, or providing the services of an outplacement agency.

With Cause

An employee may be terminated without notice, or pay in lieu of notice, when there is just cause for dismissal. However, it is best to take legal advice before dismissing for cause.

Some examples of just cause would be wilful disobedience, wilful neglect of duty, theft, fraud, dishonesty, insubordination, breach of trust, chronic lateness or absenteeism that is not corrected after warnings, misrepresenting qualifications on an application, bullying, or sexually harassing another person. While this sounds straightforward, it can be complicated. You might not have just cause to dismiss a person if you had previously condoned their behaviour, or if you had treated another person more leniently for the same offence. In cases where the conduct is not so serious as to call for immediate dismissal, the employer has the responsibility to provide reasonable warnings to the employee. Those warnings must make it clear that the individual's employment will be terminated for cause if the behaviour persists.

Notifying Others

If other employees, clients, or suppliers will be affected by the person leaving, it is important to decide how to inform them. They do not require details, just a short message advising that the employee is leaving the business effective on such-and-such a date, and the name of the person to contact for any business issues until further notice. Of course, such notice should not be sent until after the employee has been advised of their termination. Other employees will have various reactions to the news, and it is helpful to have a plan for dealing with their concerns.

The Termination Meeting

The termination meeting is widely recognized as being stressful for the employee. However, people do not realize how challenging it can be for the manager. Here are tips I received from an outplacement agency to ease the process for both parties:

> ➤ Have a second person present as a witness.

> ➤ Hold the meeting somewhere other than the manager's office. This allows the manager to leave the room after giving the unwelcome news.

> ➤ Have someone who is less personally involved deal with the employee's questions, emotions, and concerns, and give the employee time to regain composure if required. This is usually the human resources manager if there is one.

➤ Arrange seating so the manager sits between the employee and the door to allow a graceful exit and for safety if there is a risk of the employee's response becoming physical.

After the Termination Meeting

What happens after the termination meeting depends on the cirumstances. If the employee has been given working notice of termination and is expected to return to work the following day, you may wish to give them the rest of the day off so they can come to terms with the situation and consult legal counsel.

If the termination of employment is immediate, have a plan in place to deal with their exit from the premises. You might offer the employee the option to pack up personal items immediately, or to do so at an after-hours meeting with you. Escorting them to their workstation and off the premises is the prudent thing to do, but I would do so as discreetly and respectfully as possible.

Get Help if You Need It

You can use outplacement agencies or consultants for the termination process. These professionals provide a range of services, from consulting with the manager and attending the termination meeting, to offering career transitioning assistance for the employee. If needed, you can also hire someone from a security company to be in attendance.

Turnover

Employee turnover is a growing challenge for employers. You find the right candidates, spend time training them, and then they resign. A certain amount of turnover is to be expected as employees find better jobs, better pay, or have personal reasons for leaving (e.g., a spousal transfer). On the other hand, if the turnover rate is excessive, you will need to find out why people are leaving your business.

A formal exit interview can help you to identify the reasons. The best exit interviews do not just ask why the person is leaving and what the organization could have done to keep them. Asking probing questions can assist in identifying possible causes. Sample questions might include: "Did you feel that you were fairly compensated for your work? Did you find your job challenging? Did you feel that your manager treated you well? Did you have a good relationship with co-workers? Did you feel you were overworked? What can the new company offer you that we cannot?" The answers will help you to identify problems that need to be addressed.

It is helpful to conduct occasional retention interviews. By asking similar questions of existing employees, you can often identify and resolve issues before they become unmanageable.

In a retention interview, ask employees about their aspirations as well as their work and relationships with managers and co-workers. An employee might like to become a supervisor or manager. Through training and mentoring, they can be prepared for the next opportunity in your organization. It can be frustrating to lose someone who has been identified as a high performer, with potential for promotion, because the individual is not aware of your plans for them.

Providing References

You conduct background checks before hiring staff. So will other employers. Supplying a reference for a good worker is easy enough but it may be more difficult for somebody who has been terminated from your company. Refusal to provide a reference could be interpreted as a negative comment about the person but is a legitimate option.

You could discuss with the departing employee what you are prepared to say to any prospective employer. That way, there will be no surprises and the person can be prepared to address issues raised in a future interview. Any comments should be true and supported by documented evidence.

To help ensure fairness and accuracy, establish a policy that requires all reference requests to be directed to someone who has been trained in this capacity. This would normally be a human resources representative.

Administration

There is a significant amount of administrative work in human resources management. It involves, for example, maintaining electronic employee records, updating policies and procedures, answering employees' questions, and monitoring policies and practices for legal compliance. If you do not have human resources support, consider delegating the work to an administrative assistant.

Companies are to keep a current, confidential, file for each employee in a secure location. Ontario's *Employment Standards Act, 2000* defines what information must be kept for each employee and for how long. In addition to the employee's name, address, and start date, the file needs to have records of their pay, hours worked, vacations, vacation pay, leaves of absence, training records, and so on.

Other documents kept in employee files normally include a copy of the individual's résumé, social insurance number, and any documents signed when the person was hired. In addition, keep copies of any performance appraisals or disciplinary notes, and any other important information pertaining to the employment relationship.

If you offer employer-sponsored benefits, retain copies of any documents signed by employees when they accept, select, or change benefits coverage.

Employees should be aware of everything in their files, and I believe they should be able to review the information on request. With the person's knowledge, I would remove sensitive information, such as comments made by former employers or referees who expected their input to remain confidential. A manager, or a trusted third party, should be present to protect the integrity of the file.

Employee files should be current, and disciplinary records should have an expiry date. If someone responds well to a performance improvement plan and becomes a good performer, what is the value of keeping the record indefinitely?

Forms

In human resources, there is a form to fit every occasion, such as job applications, job descriptions, timecards, vacation requests, and performance reviews. You can search the internet to find professional sites that offer free, downloadable formats and templates. Alternatively, you can have a qualified consultant develop the documents you will need, ensuring the forms comply with legislation.

CHAPTER 9

Miscellaneous

This chapter includes miscellaneous topics that have not previously been discussed or fully addressed.

Controlling your reputation by developing an employer brand and understanding the importance of employee engagement are complementary to hiring and managing staff.

An overview of the job evaluation process is a supplement to the pay equity information in Chapter 1.

I have also included information for those who would like to implement a dress code, and those who want more information about unions.

While the process of hiring a human resources professional is no different from the recruitment guidelines outlined in Chapter 3, I have made some suggestions to assist you in finding the right HR person.

Finally, I have introduced The Birkman Method®, a motivational assessment tool that has had a significant impact on my personal growth.

Your Employer Brand

Will Rogers said, "It takes a lifetime to build a good reputation, but you can lose it in a minute." As on-line employee reviews demonstrate, a business can have a reputation or employer brand that can make a difference in its ability to hire and retain good people.

People want to work for a company whose values match their own. Candidates may want to know about the experiences of people who work for you: Was your recruitment process professional and welcoming? Do people enjoy working for you? Are the pay and benefits competitive? Are there opportunities for advancement or career development? Do you support employees' volunteer work?

Thanks to social media, candidates will also be aware of anything that has hurt your reputation. There is always someone with a cell phone who will record controversial situations.

Job seekers obtain information about employers from many sources: some you can control, and others you cannot.

Your website is a public-facing site for managing your employer reputation, and one you can control. When reviewing it, ask yourself the following questions. As well as advertising products and services, does it give potential employees the sense that your business is a wonderful place to work? What makes you unique?

What do you have to offer employees? Does it illustrate your involvement in the community? Are there charities that you support, and will you encourage employees to get involved? Many people want to work for a business that makes a difference and some employers post pictures of employees participating in company-sponsored charity events.

You can control the candidate and employee experience at your business. Candidates are likely to have a positive impression if you respond quickly and professionally to job applications. You will make a good impression if applicants feel welcomed when they attend an interview, and if you show respect by conducting interviews on time and staying engaged with candidates during the hiring process.

New employees are likely to think well of the business if your written job offers are exactly as discussed and there are no surprises in their actual responsibilities or working conditions. They will feel accepted if you and your co-workers make them feel welcome. A well-designed orientation program will help them to understand the environment and the requirements of their new jobs. From then on, your employer brand depends on the employees' experiences.

You cannot control word-of-mouth. Before deciding whether to apply to an advertisement, candidates can investigate your business. As well as asking friends and family, they can research your organization on-line. There, they can find customer complaints, check the Better Business Bureau for ratings, and through sites like Glassdoor, read reviews by current and former employees. It is advisable to examine these sources so you can be aware of negative customer and employee experiences.

Employee Engagement

Employee engagement goes beyond employee satisfaction. Engaged employees are people who enjoy their work and who are committed to driving the business forward. They also tend to be high performers.

One way to promote engagement is to put good front-line managers in place - managers who create mutual trust. I have had the pleasure of working in such an environment. Employees went out of their way to satisfy customers and knew that managers would support their decisions. It was easy to feel that one made a difference.

In a small business, the front-line manager is often the owner so investing in personal management coaching may be helpful.

There are companies that specialize in surveying employees to measure and improve employee engagement. The challenge with such surveys, however, is that they lead employees to expect that something will be done with the results. If people do not see the response they would like, it can lead to frustration and mistrust of the organization.

Job Evaluation

Job evaluation compares positions according to criteria which determine their relative worth to the company. Such evaluations are necessary, for example, once you have 10 employees and must comply with provincial pay equity legislation.

The evaluation process uses current and valid job descriptions to assess each position in the organization according to these criteria and to assign points, rankings, or classifications depending on the method used. This not only determines the relative value of the jobs in different departments, but also helps to determine differences in pay scales. Pay equity regulations specifically require comparison based on the criteria of skill, effort, responsibility and working conditions.

Companies can manage job evaluation themselves. The Ontario Pay Equity Commission's website provides a useful, interactive, job comparison tool. Using the tool involves choosing a set of subfactors for skill, effort, responsibility and working conditions and assigning levels and definitions to each one. Further, it involves generating a questionnaire to collect job information, adding points/weights to the system, evaluating all jobs, and comparing the jobs for pay equity.

Some companies prefer to use commercially available, well-established job evaluation systems and software, or to hire an independent consultant to do the work. An independent consultant might be less expensive but be sure to hire the right person. I was once asked to evaluate jobs using a chart designed by a consultant. In some instances, the same description had been used at different competency levels. As a result, for example, the description *enters data into a computer system under strict supervision* could be assigned either 5 points or 10 points. This duplication would not stand up to a test of validation for pay equity purposes.

Aside from assisting companies in meeting pay equity requirements, job evaluation becomes useful when the organization is large enough to need a process to maintain consistency among jobs in different departments. The evaluations promote fairness in pay structures and facilitate promotions and transfers between departments. Regression analysis can be used to assign salary ranges based on job points.

Dress Codes

A dress code may be important to you because employees represent your brand and you want them to make a good impression. Alternatively, you may want a dress code to match industry standards, to respect societal norms, or because it is a personal preference.

You are entitled to decide how you want employees to dress, as long as you do not violate Ontario's *Human Rights Code*, which states:

Employers must make sure that any uniform or dress code policy does not undermine employees' dignity and right to fully take part in the workplace because of *Code* grounds, such as sex (which includes pregnancy), race, gender identity, disability, gender expression, and creed (religion).

I suggest keeping it simple. The more detail you include, the more of a headache it could become. I once worked in an environment with very prescriptive dress rules. As the human resources representative, I received regular complaints from employees and supervisors, who seemed to think of me as the dress code police. Dealing with these issues was a non-productive use of my time as well as that of the complainants.

Putting the onus on employees to decide what is appropriate acknowledges them as mature professionals who can be trusted to do the right thing.

Note: Frequent complaints about minor issues like a dress code may be a symptom of larger problems.

Unions

In Canada, most workers have the right to form a union or to join one that already exists. Ontario requires that 40 percent of all eligible workers sign a union membership card before their union can apply to the Ontario Labour Relations Board (Board) for certification. The union is required to deliver a certification package to the employer before filing an application with the Board. Upon receipt of the certification package, the employer has two days to deliver its response to the applicant union, file a response with the Board, and post in the workplace a copy of the application for certification along with a notification to employees. The notification must inform employees of their rights, advise them that a secret ballot vote will take place, and direct them to look for future postings with more details.

The Board will then order that a vote be held among the eligible employees, usually five days after the application filing date. It will contact both the employer and the union to reach agreement on details surrounding the vote, including which employees will be eligible to join the union. This group of eligible employees is called a bargaining unit, and members are entitled to vote by secret ballot. The union may be certified if 50 percent of employees who vote do so in favour of union representation. That means that employees who do not wish to join, but fail to vote, are effectively supporting the union.

The employer does not decide the terms and conditions of employment for unionized employees but must negotiate them with the union representing the bargaining unit. The negotiation process is called *collective bargaining* and leads to a written agreement, called a *collective agreement*. This agreement sets out the employment terms and conditions for unionized employees, as well as the rights, privileges and duties of the union, employer, and employees. The union also represents members in disputes with the employer.

Because the time between the union's application and the Board's response is so short, employers can be taken by surprise when their workers decide to organize. However, an alert manager will be able to recognize certain signs. Unusual and secretive gatherings that may include strangers, an increase in employee complaints, and an unusual interest in company policies, employee handbooks, or benefits plans could be early evidence of union activity.

Companies facing a union organizing drive today should consult a lawyer with experience in labour relations. While employers have certain rights, including the right to provide employees with information, active anti-union activities could smooth the union's way to certification.

Satisfied employees may not see the need for a union and may resist any attempt to form one. In the words of a former labour relations instructor, "If you want to avoid a union drive in your company, get rid of the turkey managers."

Hiring a Human Resources Professional

Eventually, you will need help in managing the many human resources responsibilities. Initially, you might want to work with specialized consultants on an as-needed basis, depending on their areas of expertise. An on-line search for human resources consultants is a good place to start, and the list can be narrowed by adding the required specialty. For example, HR Consultant – Recruiting, HR Consultant – Talent Management.

The first human resources employee in a small organization should probably be a generalist: someone who has a solid grounding in all aspects of the human resources function including legislation and best practices. It is also important that your human resources partner understand your business and industry. As well as the appropriate education and experience, candidates should have the right soft skills. For a significant part of my career, I was a hands-on generalist, and my perspective is that the role requires analytical and communications skills, integrity, honesty, confidence, emotional intelligence, self-assurance, an open mind, and the ability to speak truth to power. As this person will have access to sensitive information, the ability to maintain confidentiality is also extremely important.

At this time it is not necessary to obtain formal qualifications to practise human resources in Canada. However, hiring a professionally certified candidate ensures you have someone in place with the right training and who is bound by rules of conduct. Two organizations provide certification in Canada.

Nationally, except in Ontario, the Chartered Professionals in Human Resources (CPHR) has member associations in nine provinces and three territories. Members who meet the qualifications earn the designation of Chartered Professional in Human Resources. For a fee, HR job openings can be posted on the websites of provincial and territorial member associations. CPHR is Canada's representative on the North American Human Resources Management Association and the World Federation of People Management Associations.

In Ontario, the Human Resources Professionals Association (HRPA) is a regulatory body under the *Registered Human Resources Professionals Act, 2013*. The HRPA job board, hireauthority.ca, is a fee-based service targeted to people in the human resources industry. Job postings are broadcast by e-mail to all members of the association. There is also a searchable public register which records members' qualifications and disciplinary history.

HRPA offers three levels of qualification: Certified Human Resources Professional (CHRP), Certified Human Resources Leader (CHRL), and Certified Human Resources Executive (CHRE). The three qualification levels are as follows:

> ➤ CHRP is an entry-level designation. You would hire someone at this level to perform clerical or administrative roles such as maintaining a HRIS,

processing payroll and benefits, conducting preliminary interviews with job applicants, updating policies and procedures, and handling correspondence.

➤ CHRL is the professional-level designation. You should look for this level of competence when hiring independent consultants or an in-house generalist or manager.

➤ HR professionals at the CHRE level must have acquired executive-level competencies in areas such as governance, business strategy, and executive compensation.

The same due diligence is needed when recruiting an HR professional as for any other employee.

The Birkman Method®

In Chapter 3, I mentioned personality assessments as a tool in recruiting. These instruments are becoming increasingly popular in the human resources field, where they are also used for leadership development, coaching, and teambuilding.

Some products are better than others. One has made such a positive impact on my life that I would like to mention it here. You may find it useful for understanding your relationships at work and elsewhere.

I was introduced to The Birkman Method® early in my career and used it in my work for teambuilding and conflict resolution. On the personal side, it was a huge contributor to my own growth in emotional intelligence.

The method was developed by Dr. Roger Birkman, who became interested in behavioural psychology during the Second World War. A bomber pilot who was shot down in Belgium and escaped through the underground, he was intrigued by the way people reacted differently to the same stressful events. After the war, he studied psychology. At a time when most psychologists were studying *abnormal* behaviour, Dr. Birkman focused his research on *normal* people. In 1951 he developed a Test of Social Comprehension on which The Birkman Method® is based, and he spent his life researching and enhancing his understanding of why people behave as they do.

Other assessments I have used explain how we differ from each other, but they leave me with a feeling of "so what?" How does knowing that I differ from others help me? The Birkman Method® goes deeper. As well as looking at normal, everyday behaviour, it delves into the kind of environment that is best for an individual, and the unproductive stress behaviours that can result when a person is immersed too long in the wrong environment. It also provides the tools and understanding for managing those unproductive stress behaviours to become more effective in working with others.

If you would like more information about Dr. Birkman and The Birkman Method® you can find it at www.birkman.com.

Useful On-Line Resources

The internet is a good place to find information for your business. A search for any topic related to employment will point you to appropriate federal, provincial, and territorial government websites as well as to postings by subject-matter experts. Government websites provide electronic and/or telephone contact information. Numbers for government departments are also listed in local telephone books.

The following on-line resources may be helpful, and the URL addresses were current at time of publication.

A copy of this resource section, with active links, is available on my website: urhr.ca

GOVERNMENT OF CANADA
The official website of the federal government is: *https://www.canada.ca*

Canada Labour Code
The CLC defines employment standards for employers in federally regulated industries (for information only as

federally regulated industries are not covered in this book).
https://laws.justice.gc.ca/eng/acts/l-2/index.html

Canada Pension Plan
The CPP website provides details of the CPP retirement pension.
https://www.canada.ca/en/services/benefits/publicpensions/cpp.html

Canada Revenue Agency
The CRA administers tax laws for the federal and provincial governments. The CRA website provides valuable information for small businesses, including registering a business, payroll administration, income tax, and GST.
https://www.canada.ca/en/revenue-agency.html

Employment and Social Development Canada – Employment Equity for Federal Contractors
Details of the Federal Contractors' Program (for employers with 100 or more employees and with government contracts of over $1 million) can be found at
https://www.canada.ca/en/employment-social-development/programs/employment-equity/federal-contractor-program.html

Employment Insurance
The EI website provides details of the EI benefit and employers' responsibilities.
https://www.canada.ca/en/services/benefits/ei.html

Federally Regulated Businesses
The federally regulated businesses and industries page of the Government of Canada website identifies those industries that are federally regulated and provides links to information about employment standards legislation in each province and territory.
https://www.canada.ca/en/employment-social-development/
programs/employment-equity/regulated-industries.html

Federal Labour Standards
The CLC establishes employment conditions and standards that apply to employees working in federally regulated businesses.
https://www.canada.ca/en/services/jobs/workplace/federal-
labour-standards.html

Government of Canada Job Bank
The Government of Canada Job Bank provides resources for both job seekers and employers. There is a job board where employers can post openings. A link to trend analyses provides information that may be helpful in defining and pricing jobs.
https://employer.jobbank.gc.ca/employer/

National Occupational Classification
The NOC is Canada's national system for describing occupations. You can search the register to find how an occupation is classified or to learn about its main duties, educational requirements, aptitudes, interests, and other useful information.

*https://www.canada.ca/en/employment-social-development/
services /noc.html*

O*Net

The U.S. Department of Labor's O*Net is similar to Canada's NOC.
https://www.onetonline.org/

Privacy

The Office of the Privacy Commissioner of Canada enforces privacy laws in Canada, including PIPEDA. At the time of this writing, PIPEDA applies in Ontario because the province does not have a law that has been deemed substantially similar to the federal legislation.
https://www.priv.gc.ca/en

Service Canada

Service Canada provides Canadians with a single point of access to a wide range of government services and benefits such as EI, CPP, Canada Pension Plan Disability (CPP-D), Old Age Security (OAS), and applications for SIN's and passports. Their website provides information about services, as well as the location of centres that are available to the public.
*https://www.canada.ca/en/employment-social-development/
corporate /portfolio/service-canada.html*

Veterans Affairs Canada Job Bank

Employers wishing to hire a veteran can post a job through this site.
https://www.jobbank.gc.ca/hiring/veterans

GOVERNMENT OF ONTARIO
The official website of the Ontario government is:
https://www.ontario.ca

Accident Reporting
Employers are required to notify the Ministry of Labour, Training and Skills Development in the event of a workplace accident or incident that results in death or injury. Details are available at
https://www.ontario.ca/page/reporting-workplace-incidents-or-structural-hazards

Accessibility for Ontarians with Disabilities Act
For information about Ontario's accessibility legislation and the *Accessibility for Ontarians with Disabilities Act* (AODA) see:
https://www.ontario.ca/page/accessibility-laws
or
https://www.aoda.ca/

Employment Standards
The *Employment Standards Act, 2000* and related information can be found at
https://www.labour.gov.on.ca/english/es/

Financial Services Regulatory Authority of Ontario
The Financial Services Regulatory Authority of Ontario (FSRA), formerly the Financial Services Commission of Ontario (FSCO), regulates financial services such as the insurance sector and pensions. The FSRA administers

Ontario's *Pension Benefits Act*.
http://www.fsco.gov.on.ca/en/Pages/default.aspx

Human Rights
For information on the *Human Rights Code*, refer to the website of the Ontario Human Rights Commission.
http://www.ohrc.on.ca/en

Ministry of Finance (Employer Health Tax)
The Ontario government levies a payroll tax on remuneration paid to employees to help fund healthcare in the province. Employers may claim a tax exemption if their total annual payroll is lower than a specified threshold.
https://www.fin.gov.on.ca/en/tax/eht/index.html

Ministry of Labour, Training and Skills Development
Ontario's Ministry of Labour, Training and Skills Development is the primary source of information for employers in the province. Here, you will find links to employment standards, occupational health and safety, and labour relations legislation as well as services provided to employers.
https://www.labour.gov.on.ca

Occupational Health and Safety
On the website of the Ministry of Labour, Training and Skills Development, you can access information about safety at work and a copy of the *Occupational Health and Safety Act*.
https://www.labour.gov.on.ca/english/hs/

Ontario Health Insurance Plan

The provincial government pays for many of the health services needed by Ontarians through OHIP.
https://www.ontario.ca/page/what-ohip-covers

Ontario Disability Support Program

The Ministry of Children, Community and Social Services provides employment assistance to people with disabilities. Assistance can include training and transportation as well as assistive devices and software.
https://www.mcss.gov.on.ca/en/mcss/programs/social/odsp/employment_support/available_Supports.aspx

Ontario Labour Relations Board

The Ontario Labour Relations Board adjudicates matters between employers and labour unions.
www.olrb.gov.on.ca

Ontario Pay Equity Commission

Private sector employers with 10 or more employees must comply with the *Pay Equity Act*. Information is available on the Ontario Pay Equity Commission's website.
http://www.payequity.gov.on.ca/en/Pages/default.aspx

Service Ontario Business Services

Employers can register a business, search the information guide, or find provincial forms and other information on the Service Ontario business services website.
https://www.ontario.ca/page/business-services

Workplace Hazardous Materials Information System
In Ontario, the Ministry of Labour, Training and Skills Development is responsible for the enforcement of both federal and provincial legislation dealing with the Workplace Hazardous Materials Information System (WHMIS).
https://www.ontario.ca/page/workplace-hazardous-materials-information-system-whmis

Workplace Safety and Insurance Board
Most employers in Ontario are required to register with the Workplace Safety and Insurance Board (WSIB), formerly known as the Workers Compensation Board (WCB). Details can be found at *https://www.wsib.ca/en*

OTHER RESOURCES

Business Training
The Canadian Management Centre provides training and information for business leaders. Its website includes a library of free resources.
https://cmcoutperform.com/home

Canadian Federation of Independent Business
The Canadian Federation of Independent Business (CFIB) provides members with an on-line toolkit for human resources policies and procedures and a business help line that includes support for human resources issues.
https://www.cfib-fcei.ca/en

Canadian Payroll Association

The Canadian Payroll Association provides free downloadable resources. A fee-based membership in the association provides employers with additional resources including updates on issues, trends, and legislation.
http://www.payroll.ca

Chartered Professionals in Human Resources

Chartered Professionals in Human Resources (CPHR) represents human resources professionals in Canada's territories, and in all provinces except Ontario. CPHR bills itself as "the national voice on the enhancement and promotion of the HR Profession."
https://cphr.ca

Employee Benefits

The Benefits Alliance Group is a small group of benefits advisors from across Canada who "provide superior advice and counsel for their clients' group insurance and retirement arrangements." While I am not familiar with the group, I learned of it through a trusted benefits advisor who is a member.
https://www.benefitsalliance.ca

Human Resources News Journals

The Canadian HR Reporter Group is an electronic format which provides a wealth of information from three industry news journals: Canadian HR Reporter, Canadian Employment Law Today, and Canadian Labour Reporter. It also offers a free subscription to a newswire service.

Subscribers are sent weekly e-newsletters with updates on the latest developments and have full access to a searchable archive of past issues.
https://www.hrreporter.com/news/hr-news

Human Resources Professionals Association
The Human Resources Professionals Association (HRPA) is a regulatory body under Ontario's *Registered Human Resources Professionals Act, 2013.* The association has a job board (Hire Authority) and e-mails job openings to all members (approximately 24,000). Potential employers of human resources professionals can also check the registration status and disciplinary history of a member.
https://www.hrpa.ca

Glossary Of Terms

The following is a list of terms as they are used in the HR field. Some are included for information only and are not addressed in this book.

absenteeism. Being absent from work. Absenteeism may be *culpable* (within the employee's control) or *non-culpable* (unavoidable).

administrative services only (ASO). An arrangement in which an organization funds its own employee benefits plan, and hires an outside consultant to perform administrative services, such as maintaining records and assessing claims.

alternative benefit year. A twelve-month period used as an alternative to a calendar year for the purpose of management and renewal of benefits contracts.

annuity. A product purchased from funds invested in an employee's retirement plan to provide a guaranteed regular income at retirement.

Accessibility for Ontarians with Disabilities Act (AODA). A provincial law designed to eliminate barriers for people who have a disability.

applicant tracking system (ATS). A software application used in recruiting. Information from applicants is uploaded to a database where it can be organized and searched by key words.

back-fill (a position). Replacing one employee with another when, for example, the first has been transferred or promoted.

background check. Investigation of a candidate's work, education, and other job-related history to confirm their qualifications for a position.

banked overtime. Overtime hours which, rather than being paid when earned, are recorded and taken as time off at a later date. See time off in lieu.

bargaining unit. A group of employees represented by a single labour union in negotiations with an employer.

base pay. The rate of pay for a job, whether hourly or salaried, excluding additional payments such as overtime or bonuses.

behavioural interview. A technique of interviewing candidates by asking questions about how they have handled situations in the past. The assumption is that past behaviour predicts future behaviour.

benchmark job. A job that has common characteristics across industries and therefore can be used to make comparisons for the purpose of salary surveys and job evaluation.

bona fide occupational requirement (BFOR). A rule or practice under the *Human Rights Code* which allows an organization to establish that a requirement, qualification, or factor is necessary for proper or efficient performance of a job. The BFOR is an exception which allows an employer to impose a rule or practice that would otherwise violate human rights legislation.

call-in pay. See reporting pay.

Canada Labour Code **(CLC).** An Act of the Parliament of Canada that establishes rules of work for employees who are subject to federal labour standards.

Canada Revenue Agency (CRA). Formerly known as Revenue Canada, this federal agency administers tax laws for the Canadian government and for most provinces and territories. Quebec has its own agency called Revenu Quebec.

cause. Conduct by an employee that is so serious that it damages the employment relationship and justifies immediate dismissal without notice. Also referred to as just cause.

certification. The process by which a labour union becomes the exclusive bargaining agent for a group of employees.

Certified Human Resources Executive (CHRE). Executive-level designation bestowed by the Human Resources Professionals Association of Ontario.

Certified Human Resources Leader (CHRL). Professional-level designation bestowed by the Human Resources Professionals Association of Ontario.

Certified Human Resources Professional (CHRP). Entry-level designation bestowed by the Human Resources Professionals Association of Ontario.

Chartered Professionals in Human Resources (CPHR). An organization that represents members of the human resources profession in provinces and territories outside Ontario. Members earn the designation of Chartered Professional in Human Resources (CPHR).

claims experience. A history of the claims filed and paid out by an insurance company or other employee benefits plan provider.

collective agreement. A written contract between an employer and a labour union, outlining the terms and conditions of employment for employees in a bargaining unit.

common law. Law derived from custom and judicial precedent rather than statutes.

compensation. The payment an employee receives in return for services provided to an employer. For example, base pay, overtime, shift differentials, commission, and bonuses are classified as compensation.

competency-based interview. A technique in which candidates answer job-based questions or complete tasks that illustrate their qualifications.

consideration. Something of value exchanged in return for a contractual agreement or granted by the employer to the employee when revising a contract.

constructive dismissal. An event that occurs when an employee resigns involuntarily as a result of an employer making a unilateral fundamental change in terms of employment or creating a hostile work environment.

Consumer Price Index (CPI). An indicator of the average change in prices paid by consumers for defined goods and services over a period of time.

contingency. The arrangement with a recruiter or employment agency whereby an employer does not pay a fee unless they hire one of the candidates referred by the recruiter or agency.

consignment. An arrangement in which an employer hires a recruiter or employment agency to conduct a search for candidates on the employer's behalf.

contribution holiday. A period of time when an employer does not make payments into the pension fund of its employees.

coordination of benefits. A provision that determines the sequencing of coverage when plan members and their dependents are eligible under more than one benefits plan. For example, where each spouse has dependent coverage under a company-sponsored plan, costs not covered by the employee's plan may be submitted to the spouse's plan.

cost of living adjustment (COLA). An increase in income that reflects the cost of living as defined by a metric such as the Consumer Price Index.

deductible. The amount of money one must pay out of pocket before a claim may be submitted to an insurance plan.

dependent contractor. A contractor that is economically dependent on one principal or employer. Where a dependent contractor relationship exists, the relationship will be akin to an employment relationship and the employer may be liable to provide notice of termination.

direct compensation. Any pay made directly and regularly to an employee, such as salary, commission, bonus, overtime pay, and vacation pay.

disability. A physical or mental condition that limits a person's capacity to perform any or all requirements of a job.

discrimination. The unjust or prejudicial treatment of people. In particular, the unjust treatment of categories of people on grounds prohibited by Ontario's *Human Rights Code*.

dismissal. Unilateral termination of a worker's employment by the employer.

dismissal for cause. Termination of employment by the employer due to the employee's misconduct, disobedience, neglect of duty, or other serious breach of the terms of employment.

dress code. A set of rules specifying the required manner of dress at work.

duty to accommodate (Human Rights). An employer's responsibility to modify the duties and/or conditions of employment to assist a qualified person with respect to any protected ground under human rights legislation, so the person may successfully complete assigned work.

employee assistance plan (EAP). An employee benefit that provides a confidential, short-term counselling service for employees with personal problems that may affect their work performance.

employee development plan. A process put in place to help an employee to enhance proficiency or gain new skills.

employer-sponsored benefit. A form of compensation provided in addition to salary or wages, used to attract and retain employees. Also known as supplementary benefit.

emotional intelligence. The ability to recognize emotions and their impact on one's own or others' behaviour, and to be in control of one's own emotions.

employee handbook. A publication provided to employees by their employers, which outlines important company information, policies, and procedures.

Employment Standards Act, 2000 **(ESA).** Ontario legislation that establishes the minimum standards for working in the province and defines the rights of employees and employers. Other provinces and territories have their own employment standards acts or codes.

entrepreneur. A person who establishes a business. While this can mean any type of business, the focus of this book is to assist those who are sole entrepreneurs or small business owners.

exception hourly. A term used in reference to employees who work and are paid the same number of hours each week. Adjustments for unusual events such as time off or overtime are made retroactively, in the first pay period following the event.

experience-rated benefits programs. Employee benefits plans in which the premiums paid to the provider are established based on the actual claims experience of the insured group (i.e. cost of claims incurred in previous years).

executive compensation. Pay and benefits earned by executives of a company, usually structured so that a significant portion of compensation is at risk, meaning tied to the accomplishment of specific goals.

Federal Contractors Program (FCP). Requires that certain contractors who do business with the Canadian government achieve and maintain a workforce that is representative of the Canadian workforce. This includes members of four designated groups: women, aboriginal peoples, members of visible minorities, and persons with disabilities.

first payor. The primary benefits provider. When an employee is eligible for benefits coverage from more than one source (e.g., spouse's employer), a claim is submitted to the first payor for settlement. Any amount not covered by the first payor may then be submitted to the alternate payor.

forced ranking. An employee performance evaluation practice in which managers are required to slot a certain percentage of employees into each of several levels of performance rating. Also known as stacked ranking.

full-time employment. Employment based on a full work week as established by the employer. Typically defined as 30 to 40 hours per week.

fundamental change in terms of employment. Any adjustment to an employment relationship in which the terms of employment are changed significantly. Examples include a change of hours or pay, relocation, or a major change in roles and responsibilities.

group rates. The insurance rates (premiums) available through an insurance plan that combines individuals into one group plan. Spreading the risk over a large number of people allows the insurer to offer lower premiums.

harassment. Engaging in a course of vexatious comment or conduct that is known or ought reasonably to be known to be unwelcome.

home worker. See remote worker.

hourly employment. Employment in which employees are paid an hourly wage for the number of hours worked.

hours of work. The number of hours in which one engages in paid work.

human resources (HR). Formerly referred to as Personnel. The people who make up the workforce in an organization. Also refers to the department responsible for the people side of a business.

human resource(s) information system (HRIS). Software used to store and manipulate job-related information about employees.

human resources business partner. A human resources professional who works closely with an organization's senior leaders to develop a human resources agenda that closely supports the overall aims of the organization.

Human Resources Professionals Association (HRPA). An association that, under Ontario's *Registered Human Resources Professionals Act, 2013*, governs and regulates the professional practice of registered members in the province.

Human Rights Code. Ontario's legislation that prohibits discrimination against people on protected grounds that include age, ancestry, colour, race, citizenship, ethnic origin, place of origin, creed, disability, family status, marital status (including single status), gender identity, gender expression, receipt of public assistance (in housing only), record of offences (in employment only), sex (including pregnancy and breastfeeding), and sexual orientation. The federal government, other provinces, and the three territories have similar legislation.

incumbent. The person currently occupying a position.

independent contractor. A person who is hired to deliver a product or service and has full control over how the work is accomplished. An independent contractor is not an employee of the contracting organization.

indirect compensation. Non-monetary benefits, such as life and health insurance and retirement benefits, provided to an employee.

insured benefits. Employee benefits provided through a contract with a third party, such as an insurance company.

job analysis. A detailed examination of the characteristics of a job in order to understand the job.

job description. A written outline of the duties, purpose, responsibilities, scope, and working conditions of a specific job.

just cause. See cause.

knowledge-based economy. An economy based on the production, distribution, and use of knowledge and information.

Labour Relations Act, 1995 (LRA). The statute that regulates labour relations and collective bargaining in unionized workplaces in Ontario. Other provinces have their own labour relations acts or codes.

leave of absence. An absence from work that has the approval of management.

legislated benefit. An employee benefit that employers must provide by law, such as the CPP, EI, and certain leaves of absence.

lieu pay. See pay in lieu of notice.

Life Income Fund (LIF). A type of registered retirement income fund used to hold, and pay out, locked-in retirement funds.

Locked-in Retirement Account (LIRA). A registered account that holds vested pension funds for an employee who has left the sponsoring employer. Funds cannot be accessed until an approved date such as the employee's normal retirement date.

long-term. Occurring over a long period of time. In terms of disability, the employee may be unable to return to work for many months or years, or the disability may become permanent.

manager. A person responsible for financial, material, and/or human resources and for aligning their department with the company's overall goals.

market rate. The average or median rate of pay for people doing similar work in similar industries in the same region of the country.

Material Safety Data Sheet (MSDS). See Safety Data Sheet.

maternity leave. See pregnancy leave.

mission. In the context of this book, what a business owner wants to accomplish (i.e., the reason for the business's existence).

National Occupational Classification (NOC). A national system for describing Canadian occupations. The NOC is maintained by Employment and Social Development Canada.

notice period. The period between when notice of termination of employment is given, and the effective date of termination. Notice may be given by either the employer or the employee (i.e., resignation).

Occupational Health and Safety Act (OHSA). Ontario's legislation which sets out the health and safety rights and duties of all parties in the workplace, as well as the procedures for dealing with workplace hazards and enforcement as needed. Other Canadian jurisdictions have similar legislation.

onboarding. The process of integrating a new employee into the business.

on-call pay. Compensation paid to employees who are not at work, but who are holding themselves available for work at a moment's notice.

orientation. The process of introducing new employees to their responsibilities, co-workers, policies, procedures, and expectations.

outplacement. Support services provided to help exiting employees find new jobs, usually when they have been terminated without cause.

outplacement agency/company. A third-party organization, usually paid by the employer, to help terminated employees find new work.

overtime. Time worked beyond defined daily and weekly limits (in Ontario, hours worked in excess of 44 hours per week).

parental leave. A legislated leave of absence provided to employees when they become new parents through birth or adoption.

part-time employment. Employment based on less than a full work week. Typically, 30 or fewer hours per week.

pay in lieu of notice. Payment made to an employee who has been given notice of termination but is not required to work during the applicable notice period.

pay scale/range. A system that determines the different levels of pay for a job, based on criteria such as an employee's experience. A pay scale or range usually has a minimum, midpoint, and maximum.

pay equity. Equal pay for work of equal value. Ontario's *Pay Equity Act* requires that employers with 10 or more employees achieve pay equity between jobs held predominantly by males and those held predominantly by females.

pension deficit/shortfall. A situation that occurs when there are insufficient funds in a pension plan to cover all the obligations of the plan.

pension surplus. A situation that occurs when the value of the assets of a pension fund exceed the value of its liabilities.

pension vesting. Vesting occurs at the point in an employer-sponsored retirement plan when an employee is entitled to the full benefit of their plan, including contributions made by the employer on their behalf.

people analytics. The use of data to analyze an organization's problems or opportunities as they relate to employees. Turnover rates, time to hire, and revenue per employee are examples of people analytics metrics.

performance improvement plan. A tool to help a struggling employee meet company expectations and to document performance issues.

personal day. A paid or unpaid day of leave from work for reasons other than illness or vacation.

Personal Health Information Protection Act, 2004 **(PHIPA).** Ontario's legislation that ensures the privacy of personal health information, including that obtained by employers.

Personal Information Protection and Electronic Documents Act **(PIPEDA).** Federal legislation that protects personal information collected, used, or disclosed in the course of commercial activities.

personality assessment. In this book, a tool for evaluating candidates to determine behavioural traits that may predict job success. Also used for employee development.

plan sponsor. The entity, usually an employer, which establishes a benefit or retirement plan.

pooled benefit. An employee benefit, such as life insurance, in which the insurer groups the premiums of many sponsors together to create a large fund (pool) from which claims are paid. Premium rates for the entire group are determined by the overall claims experience of the pool.

pregnancy leave. A legislated leave of absence granted a pregnant employee prior to and following the birth of a child.

premiums. The amount paid to a third-party provider to pay for employee benefits.

pre-tax basis. Before tax is calculated. Any deduction taken from an employee on a pre-tax basis reduces the amount of pay on which income tax is calculated.

prima facie. Accepted as correct until proven otherwise.

prohibited grounds of discrimination. The specific grounds on which an employer is forbidden to discriminate against employees, according to Ontario's *Human Rights Code.*

public holiday. A paid day off that most workers in Ontario are entitled to take, as legislated by either the federal or provincial government. Employees who agree to work on a public holiday are entitled to additional compensation as prescribed by legislation. Also known as a statutory holiday.

public holiday pay. The amount paid to an employee in Ontario who is not working on a public holiday. Calculated as the average regular wages over the last 4 weeks before the holiday divided by 20.

reasonable notice. The amount of warning an employer must provide to an employee when changing or terminating an employment contract.

record of employment (ROE). A form submitted to Service Canada when an employee leaves a company for any reason. It records the employment history, reason for leaving, and EI insurable earnings. An ROE may be submitted on paper, or electronically through a Service Canada account.

recruiting. The process of attracting and employing new people to work for a company or organization.

referral bonus. Payment made to an existing employee who refers a candidate ultimately hired by the employer.

referee. A person who confirms a candidate's qualifications for a job.

reference check. The process of contacting previous employers or others to confirm a candidate's work history and suitability for a job.

regression analysis. A statistical technique that predicts the level of one variable based on the level of another variable. Used in job evaluation and analysis to determine the relative value of jobs.

regulatory body. An organization that makes rules and sets standards for an industry or profession and has direct or indirect enforcement authority or responsibility over its members.

remote worker. Also known as home worker. An employee who works from their own residence or another location. Legislation covering employees at your premises also applies to remote workers.

reporting pay. Employees who are called in to work outside of their regularly scheduled hours must receive a minimum of three hours' pay.

restrictive covenant. An agreement that requires one party to either take or abstain from a specific action. In an employment contract, a restrictive covenant may be used to prohibit an employee from competing with an employer or soliciting the employer's clients/customers for a period of time after leaving the company.

Safety Data Sheet (SDS). A document that lists all relevant information about the safety and use of a substance or product. A requirement of the Workplace Hazardous Materials Information System (WHMIS).

salaried employee. An employee who is paid a fixed amount at regular intervals for work performed.

salary continuance. The practice of continuing to pay an ex-employee's salary and benefits during the notice period after termination of employment, without requiring the employee to continue working.

salary range. The range of compensation an employer is prepared to pay for a given job within the organization. A range typically has a minimum, midpoint, and maximum.

self-administered benefit. An employee benefit in which coverage is provided directly by the employer, rather than through a third party such as an insurance company.

severance pay. Compensation, as defined by Ontario's employment standards legislation, that is to be paid "to a qualified employee who has worked for the company for at least five years, who has their employment "severed" by a company in Ontario with a payroll of at least $2.5 million, or which severed the employment of

50 or more employees within a six month period because all or part of the business permanently closed." Severance pay is required in addition to termination pay.

shift differential. Extra pay received by employees for working undesirable shifts such as nights and weekends.

short-term. Occurring over a short period of time. In terms of disability, the employee is expected to recover and return to regular duties.

sick days/sick time. The number of days per year for which an employer agrees to pay workers who are unable to work because of illness.

situational interview. A technique in which candidates are asked how they would respond to hypothetical job-related situations.

soft skills. Character traits and interpersonal skills that define how someone relates to others and to their work environment. Examples include work ethic, communication, problem solving, and teamwork.

stacked ranking. See forced ranking.

statutory holiday. See public holiday.

stock option. The right to buy a specific number of shares of company stock at a pre-set price for a fixed period of time. Often offered as an incentive to executives or highly valued employees.

succession planning. A process in which companies identify and mentor future leaders within the organization, so that they can replace senior leaders who leave the business or who are transferred or promoted.

supervisor. An employee who monitors and regulates other employees in the performance of assigned tasks, and who makes recommendations on hiring, promotions, and discipline.

supplementary benefit. See employer-sponsored benefit.

systemic discrimination. A business practice, policy, or program that inadvertently creates a disadvantage for a class of people, especially those protected by human rights legislation.

T4. A statement of earnings for income tax purposes.

talent acquisition. The process of recruiting, interviewing, and tracking job candidates plus onboarding and training those who are hired.

talent acquisition software. Software designed to support a variety of recruiting functions including sourcing, selecting, engaging, onboarding, and training.

talent management. Refers to the business strategy around recruiting, hiring, retaining, and developing the best employees.

talent pool. (a) The qualified people who are available to be chosen to fill a job opening; (b) a file or database of a recruiter's candidates.

team leader. An experienced employee who provides guidance, support, and direction to a group or team of individuals. Team leaders usually have no supervisory responsibilities.

temporary layoff. The temporary cut-back or cessation of an individual's employment with the understanding that the employee will be recalled within a certain period.

termination (of employment). The end of a person's employment with a company, whether voluntary or involuntary.

termination pay. Pay that is provided in place of notice of termination of employment. Termination pay may cover both statutory notice and common law notice periods.

time off in lieu (TOIL). Paid time off granted to an employee in place of overtime pay for excess hours worked. See banked overtime.

total cash compensation. The total value of base plus variable pay (bonus and commission).

total compensation. The total value of salary, bonus, commission, long-term incentives, and all benefits.

total direct compensation. Total annual cash compensation (including bonus and commission) plus the annualized value of long-term incentives such as stock options.

turnover/employee turnover. A measure of the number or percentage of workers who leave the company and are replaced with new employees.

undue hardship. An action requiring such significant difficulty or expense to the operation of an employer's business that it is recognized by human rights legislation as a valid reason not to provide accommodation to an employee based on a prohibited ground.

unjust dismissal. A situation in which employment is terminated by the employer and such termination breaches one or more terms of the contract or a statute provision or rule in employment law (i.e., common law). The unlawful termination of an employment contract without proper notice.

union organizing drive. The first steps taken by a union to encourage employees of a company to form or join a union.

vacation. A leave of absence for the purpose of recreation or personal time.

vacation pay. A percentage of an employee's gross earnings earned during a vacation entitlement year. It is usually paid just prior to the employee taking vacation time that has been earned. Alternatively, with the employee's written agreement, vacation pay may be paid on each pay day as it accrues.

variable compensation (variable pay). Compensation that is dependent on certain factors. It includes bonus, commission, and any portion of pay that is subject to the achievement of agreed conditions.

values. In the context of this book, the ethics and beliefs that define how a company operates.

vision. In the context of this book, an owner's concept of the future of the business.

working notice of termination. Notice given by an employer that a worker's employment will end on a future date. The employee is required to continue working until the termination date. Employers who do not provide such notice are required to provide payment in lieu of notice.

Workplace Hazardous Materials Information System (WHMIS). Canada's national hazard communication standard. In Ontario, WHMIS is administered by the provincial Ministry of Labour, Training and Skills Development.

workplace violence. Violence, or the threat of violence, against workers. It is prohibited by Ontario's *Human Rights Code*.

wrongful dismissal. See unjust dismissal.

About the Author

Pamela Urie developed her human resources and business acumen with a major Canadian chartered bank and as a member of the Canadian leadership team of a Fortune 1000 medical instrument company.

Pam served as secretary, vice president, and president of the Oakville and District Personnel Association between 1988 and 1996. She was also a member of the Human Resources Professionals Association (HRPA) from 1990 to 2015, attaining the designation of Certified Human Resources Leader (CHRL). Pam served as secretary of the Halton chapter of HRPA in 1996, was an active member of the Grand Valley chapter from 2007 to 2015, and volunteered with the HRPA Hotline in 2015, providing advice and counsel to members.

Recognizing that many small businesses in Canada did not have human resources support, Pam established a freelance consultancy in 2013. With more than 30 years' experience as a hands-on HR practitioner and manager, Pam was uniquely qualified to assist clients with recruiting, job descriptions, policy development, legislative compliance, teambuilding, and more.

In this book, *From Entrepreneur to Employer*, Pam draws on her background and experience to help new employers understand their human resources obligations and challenges. The author also provides HR reference material on her website: urhr.ca